MAKE AN EXTRA $100 THIS WEEK

PUT MORE MONEY IN YOUR POCKET WITHOUT STARTING A BUSINESS

MAYA ELLE

This book is intended for informational and educational purposes only. While every effort has been made to ensure the accuracy of the information provided, the author makes no guarantees regarding earnings or financial results. Individual outcomes will vary based on personal circumstances, effort, experience, and other factors beyond the author's control.

The author is not a financial advisor, accountant, attorney, or tax professional. Readers should seek appropriate professional advice before making financial, legal, tax, or business decisions.

CONTENTS

INTRODUCTION

If you picked up this book, chances are you're not dreaming about becoming a millionaire by next year. You're trying to solve a much more immediate problem. You need an extra $100.

Maybe your electric bill is due before payday. Maybe your car is running on fumes and you need enough to fill the tank. Maybe your kid needs money for a school field trip, your prescription costs more than you expected, or an unexpected repair just wiped out the little cushion you had. It could be groceries, a copay at the doctor's office, a birthday gift you forgot to budget for, or simply avoiding an overdraft fee before your paycheck hits.

Whatever brought you here, you're not looking for a five-year financial plan or another lecture about building passive income. You don't need someone telling you to quit your job, start a business, or build an online empire.

You need real money. You need it soon. You need ideas that actually fit into real life.

That's what this book is about.

Anyone who's ever sat at the kitchen table on a Tuesday night, calculator in hand, trying to figure out which bill can wait until Friday knows this feeling. And then it happens again the next Tuesday. And the Tuesday after that.

Being short on money isn't usually one dramatic financial disaster. It's a low, constant hum of stress that follows you everywhere. It's checking your bank balance before buying groceries. It's hoping your gas tank lasts until payday. It's wondering whether you can afford to say yes when your child brings home a permission slip for a field trip that costs twenty dollars. It's knowing exactly how much is in your account before you swipe your debit card.

Most of us have a number in our head that would make life feel a little more manageable. For some people it's thousands of dollars. But for most of us, on most weeks, it's much smaller. It's the gap between what's in the bank and what's due before your next paycheck. It's enough to top off the tank, clear a past-due notice, or keep an unexpected expense from turning into a crisis. It's the amount that lets you stop doing mental math every time you spend ten dollars.

Here's something I believe more than almost anything else when it comes to money: **a small goal that's actually accomplished beats a huge goal that's always "someday."**

Lots of people dream about starting a business, becoming financially independent, or making six figures with the perfect side hustle. There's nothing wrong with those goals. But they don't solve the problem you have this week.

Making an extra $100 does.

That hundred dollars may not change your life forever, but it can change this week. It can keep the lights on. It can fill your refrigerator. It can pay for flea medication for your dog, cover your phone bill, or keep your checking account out of the red.

And because it's real, it does something else that's just as important: it proves that you're capable of earning money outside of your regular paycheck.

I've spent years trying different ways to earn extra money, sometimes because I genuinely needed it and other times because I simply wanted to know what actually worked. Some ideas paid off almost immediately. Others were not worth the time or effort. But even the ones that failed taught me something I was able to use to make money later. I'll be honest about all of it.

But before we go any further, I want you to hear one thing. The specific method matters far less than most people think. People spend months looking for the perfect side hustle when what they really need is to pick one reasonable opportunity and start. Someone who has truly decided to make extra money almost always finds a way, with or without this book.

These pages aren't a secret formula. They're proof that there are far more opportunities than most people realize, and that taking action matters far more than finding the "perfect" idea.

So why $100 instead of $1,000 or $10,000?

Because $100 feels possible.

It doesn't require quitting your job, taking out a business loan, buying expensive equipment, or learning an entirely new career. It's a goal you can realistically reach using the time, skills, and resources you probably already have. But it's also large enough to make a real impact. It can solve an immediate problem. More importantly, it can change how you see yourself.

Once you've earned an extra $100 that you didn't have last week, something shifts. You stop wondering whether it's possible for someone like you to make extra money. You already know the answer, because you've done it.

That's the real goal of this book.

It’s not just about earning an extra hundred dollars. It’s about gaining the confidence that comes from proving to yourself that you can earn extra money when you need it.

This isn't a book about hustle culture. It's not about working eighty-hour weeks or turning every hobby into a business. It's about getting unstuck this week with what you already have, starting exactly where you are.

Before we get into specific ways to make money, we’re going to take an honest look at what may be holding you back. Not in a vague, motivational way, but in practical terms. We’ll look at the excuses that sound completely reasonable, the fears that disguise themselves as logic, and the habits and thought patterns that quietly keep people from taking the first step. Because for most people, the problem isn’t a lack of opportunities. It’s that something gets in the way before they ever try.

After that, we’ll get practical. I’ll walk you through real ways to earn extra money, including methods I’ve tried myself, what worked, what didn’t, and what I learned along the way. Some ideas will fit your life immediately. Others won’t, and that’s okay. The goal is to give you options, help you find what works for you, and inspire you to take action.

My hope is that before you finish this book, you'll come up with opportunities that fit your own life even better than the ones I've included. That wouldn't mean this book failed. It would mean it did exactly what it was supposed to do.

Let's start by getting out of your own way.

CHAPTER 1
WHAT'S REALLY HOLDING YOU BACK

Let me ask you something.

If you could put an extra $100 in your pocket this week without starting a business, learning a brand-new skill, or completely changing your schedule, would you do it?

Of course you would. Almost everyone says yes immediately.

So why haven't you?

That's a harder question to answer, because the answer usually isn't what we think it is. Most people immediately point to time. They say they're already too busy. Others point to money, convincing themselves they need money before they can make money. Some believe they don't have any skills people would actually pay for. Those explanations sound reasonable, and sometimes they even feel true. But after spending years trying different ways to earn extra income, I've become convinced that they usually aren't the real reasons people stay stuck.

The real problem is fear.

Not dramatic, movie-villain fear. Quiet fear. The kind that disguises itself as common sense. *What if I waste my time? What if nobody wants what I'm offering? What if I fail? What if I look stupid?* Those thoughts don't feel emotional. They feel practical, which is exactly why they're so convincing. We accept them as facts instead of recognizing them for what they really are: stories that keep us from taking the first step.

Before long, another week goes by. The bills are still there, the bank account hasn't changed, and we're telling ourselves we'll do something next week. Then next week becomes next month. Then, somehow, another year has passed.

1.1 THE COMFORT ZONE IS A LIAR

Here's something I've realized over the years: the comfort zone isn't actually comfortable.

There's nothing comfortable about wondering whether you'll have enough money to cover everything this month. There's nothing comfortable about checking your bank account before buying groceries or hoping your gas tank makes it until payday. There's nothing comfortable about lying awake at night running the same numbers over and over, looking for an answer that wasn't there the first three times you did the math.

The comfort zone simply feels familiar.

Our brains have an incredible ability to confuse familiar with safe. That's why people stay in jobs they don't enjoy for years. They complain about the work, dread Monday mornings, and know they're capable of something better, yet they stay because the known feels less risky than the unknown. It's not laziness. It's not a lack of ambition. It's human nature.

Psychologists call this *status quo bias*, our tendency to stick with our current situation simply because it's our current situation.

Even when another option would probably leave us better off, our brains naturally lean toward what's familiar. Understanding that changed the way I look at hesitation. Instead of asking myself, *Why am I hesitating?* I started asking, *Is this actually risky, or does it just feel uncomfortable because it's new?* Those are very different questions.

The comfort zone has another trick that's even more dangerous. It convinces you that you'll start next week.

I'll look into it this weekend.

I'll wait until work settles down.

I'll do it after vacation.

We've all said those things. The problem is that life rarely settles down on its own. There will always be another busy week, another unexpected expense, another reason to wait. If we're always waiting for the perfect time, we'll spend our entire lives waiting.

You don't need a completely different life to make an extra $100.

You just need to make one different decision.

1.2 THE STORY YOU'RE TELLING YOURSELF

Everyone who stays stuck has a story. A specific, convincing narrative about why their situation is different, why this week isn't the right week, why the usual options won't work for them.

Maybe yours sounds something like this:

I don't have time for anything extra right now.

I don't have any skills anyone would actually pay for.

I don't want to sell my stuff to strangers, that's not me.

I tried something once before and it didn't work out.

I'm too old to be starting something new.

I'm too inexperienced for anyone to take me seriously.

I have told myself versions of almost every one of these.

The first time I truly needed to find a way to make extra money was when I was in graduate school. My schedule was packed with classes, studying, assignments, and everything else that came with trying to earn a graduate degree. I remember looking at my calendar and thinking there couldn't possibly be a job that would fit into the few open spaces I had left.

So I researched.

I compared jobs, looked at different possibilities, and tried to figure out which opportunity would work perfectly with my schedule. I told myself I was being responsible and making an informed decision. But the longer I researched, the clearer it became that I wasn't really looking for the right opportunity.

I was procrastinating.

Researching allowed me to feel like I was doing something without taking the risk of actually doing it. As long as I was still comparing options, I didn't have to apply for anything. I didn't have to worry about being rejected, choosing the wrong job, or finding out that balancing work and graduate school might be difficult.

Eventually, I got tired of thinking about it. I picked one type of job I was willing to do and applied to four different openings. One of them ended up fitting my schedule perfectly, and it worked out better than I expected.

Years later, I had to lean on that same lesson after I lost my job.

The paycheck stopped, but the bills didn't. The rent had to be paid. The utilities were still due. I still needed to eat. I could spend my days worrying about what might happen, but worrying wasn't going to create income or put money in my bank account.

Once again, I had to make a decision. I was going to find a way forward, even if I couldn't see the entire path yet. Instead of looking for reasons different opportunities wouldn't work, I had to start looking for the ones that might.

Those two experiences taught me something I have never forgotten: the hardest part usually isn't making the money. The hardest part is getting past the story you have been telling yourself long enough to take the first step.

That doesn't mean those stories are ridiculous. They aren't. The exhaustion is real. The doubt you have about your own skills is genuine. The discomfort you feel about selling something, applying for a job, or putting yourself out there is not made up. I'm not going to tell you that any of these concerns are silly, and I'm not going to pretend they disappear because someone tells you to think positively.

But here is what I will tell you: **the story is not always the same thing as the truth**. It is an interpretation of your circumstances, often built out of fear and repeated so many times that it eventually starts to feel like fact.

Let's take a few of these stories apart, because they deserve more than a dismissive pep talk.

I don't have time. Most weeks already feel full before you add anything to them. But it's worth noticing something most of us already know deep down: we tend to find time for whatever we've actually decided is important. A last-minute trip to help a friend, an emergency doctor's appointment, staying late at the job we already have, an invitation we don't want to turn down, a show we're determined to finish, or thirty minutes that somehow disappear watching puppy videos, strangers dancing, or your friend's perfectly curated Instagram life. Somehow, there's always room for the things we've already decided are worth making time for. Time isn't actually the obstacle most people think it is.

I don't have any skills anyone would pay for. This one feels true and almost never is. Here's a way to test it. Imagine your car got towed, it costs $100 to get it out of the impound lot, and you absolutely must have it to get to work tomorrow. I'm convinced you'd find a way to come up with that cash. You'd sell something, ask someone, do something uncomfortable, figure out an option you've never had to consider before, because suddenly it mattered enough. You wouldn't need this book, and you wouldn't need a single new skill. The skills were never really the issue.

I don't want to sell my stuff to strangers. This one is interesting, because notice what just happened. Nobody told you that you had to sell anything to anyone. You came up with that objection on your own, before you'd even tried a single thing. That's worth sitting with for a second, because it's a pretty good example of how this works. The mind reaches for a reason to stop before it's even taken a step. If selling your stuff to strangers genuinely isn't for you, fine, there's more than one way to get to $100 in this book. But it's worth asking yourself honestly whether that's a real preference or just the first excuse that showed up, before you even gave yourself a chance to say yes.

I tried something before and it didn't work. This one carries more weight than it should because we tend to treat one attempt like a final verdict instead of what it actually was: one try, under whatever conditions happened to be true at the time. Maybe the timing was off. Maybe you didn't stick with it long enough to know either way. Maybe it simply wasn't the right fit for you, which says nothing about whether something else would work. The real mistake is treating "trying something" and "getting the result" as the same commitment. One unsuccessful attempt doesn't mean you don't have what it takes. It only means that particular approach didn't work. Almost everyone who has succeeded at anything had to try more than once. What carried them through wasn't any single attempt. It was staying committed to the result even as individual attempts came and went.

I'm too old to be starting something new. Here's the question worth asking: what is the right age, exactly? Whatever number you're picturing, there will always be a version of you a year or five years from now wishing you had started today. If you believe you're too old now, waiting won't make you feel any younger. It will only give you a bigger number to use as the same excuse. That's the trap. The belief doesn't disappear on its own. It follows you year after year until you decide that your age is not a reason to keep standing still. Nothing changes until you stop asking whether it's too late and start anyway.

I'm too inexperienced for anyone to take me seriously. This usually comes from comparing yourself to people who are already several steps ahead and forgetting that they had to start somewhere too. You picture a future version of yourself with more experience, more proof, and a stronger track record, then wait for that version to appear before taking action. But that version of you can only be built by doing the thing you haven't tried yet. Experience isn't something you gain before you begin. It comes from beginning. Almost everyone who looks experienced now once stood where you are, with very little to point to except a willingness to take the first step.

The first job of this chapter is to help you separate the story from the truth. Until you do that, no amount of practical advice, no list of money-making ideas, and no step-by-step plan will move you forward. You'll read it, nod along, and then return to the same quiet math at the kitchen table.

1.3 WHAT STAYING STUCK REALLY COSTS YOU

We talk a lot about the risk of trying something new and what it takes to change our circumstances. We rarely talk honestly about the cost of not trying.

Remaining exactly where you are, week after week, is not a neutral choice. It has a price. You feel it in the stress that hits when an unexpected expense arrives and there is no cushion to absorb it. You feel it in the resentment that builds when your financial life depends entirely on one paycheck. You see it in the opportunities, both large and small, that pass while you wait to feel ready. And the longer you wait, the more those costs begin to add up. A month becomes a year. One missed opportunity becomes several. The situation you hoped would somehow improve on its own starts to feel more permanent. Perhaps the greatest cost is never meeting the version of yourself you could become because you never gave yourself a real chance to discover what you can do.

There is another cost that is easy to miss because it doesn't look like a cost at all. It is the energy you spend worrying about money without ever moving toward a solution.

It's lying awake doing calculations you have already done a dozen times. It's feeling the weight of a bill without reaching the point where you ask, "Okay, what can I actually do about this?" That loop is exhausting in a way that never appears on a bank statement, and it can continue for months or even years without producing a single dollar of relief.

This is the part that almost never gets said plainly: **worry by itself has never paid a bill.**

You can spend an hour lying awake, running the numbers and feeling the full weight of the situation. At the end of that hour, the amount in your account hasn't changed. The bill is still there. Nothing has moved except your energy, which is now lower than it was before.

That hour didn't protect you from anything. It didn't prepare you for anything. It simply cost you an hour, along with whatever that stress did to your sleep, your mood, and the people around you who can tell something is wrong even when you don't say it out loud.

The effects of that worry build slowly, which makes them easy to overlook. One bad night may barely register. But months or years of repeating the same cycle can create a low-level exhaustion that follows you into everything else.

It affects your patience with the people you love. It makes it harder to enjoy good moments without the worry creeping back in. Over time, even a manageable financial situation can feel much bigger when you're already worn down from worrying about it.

None of that appears on a bank statement either. But it is just as real a cost as the bill that is still sitting there unpaid.

I'm not telling you this to scare you. I'm telling you because this cost rarely gets discussed, and you deserve to see the full picture before deciding that staying where you are is the safer choice.

1.4 WHAT FEAR IS ACTUALLY TELLING YOU

Here is a shift in perspective that changed the way I think about fear.

Fear is not always a stop sign. Sometimes it is a signal.

When you feel that knot in your stomach about trying something new, your brain is not necessarily telling you that the idea is bad or that you are going to fail. It may simply be telling you that the outcome matters. The situation is real enough to have consequences, and some part of you cares about what happens.

You don't usually feel that kind of fear about things that mean nothing to you. You feel it when you are considering something that might actually change your situation.

I have felt that exact knot more times than I can count, including in several of the situations this book will walk you through. It was the heart-racing, second-guessing, almost-talked-myself-out-of-it kind of fear.

Each time, the fear had less to do with actual danger and more to do with the possibility of looking foolish, embarrassing myself, or having the people around me question why I was doing it. But there was also the possibility that something could be different. It was a small crack in the wall of what had always felt familiar.

The fear wasn't proof that I should stop. It was proof that I was doing something that mattered enough to make me uncomfortable.

That distinction sounds simple, but it becomes useful once it settles in. If fear is a signal rather than a final verdict, feeling afraid is no longer evidence that you shouldn't try. It is simply a feeling you can acknowledge without allowing it to make the decision for you.

Whatever brought you to this book, whether it was a bill due sooner than you would like, the stress of being short again, or the quiet feeling that there has to be another way through this particular week, you do not have to wait until every uncomfortable feeling disappears before you begin.

1.5 THE PERMISSION YOU'VE BEEN WAITING FOR

I want to be direct about something many books in this space tend to dance around.

You do not need to have everything figured out before you begin. You also do not need to completely change your mindset, eliminate every doubt, or suddenly become a more confident version of yourself.

You do not need to know which option is right for you. You do not need to feel ready or be completely certain that something will work. You do not have to solve the time problem, the skills problem, the selling problem, or every other concern in your head before taking a single step.

You also don't have to make any of the big decisions people tend to associate with earning more money. You don't need to write a business plan, learn an entirely new skill set, quit your job, or read ten more books about financial freedom. You can still have doubts, questions, and fears.

For now, you only need to make one decision: you are going to earn an extra $100 this week.

That's it. Nothing bigger than that.

You are simply deciding that staying exactly where you are is no longer your only option. This doesn't require a dramatic transformation or a life-changing burst of motivation. It can begin with a quiet, firm decision that coming up short again is not going to be the end of this story.

So before you go any further, ask yourself honestly: Have you decided that doing nothing is no longer an option?

Can you commit right now to making an extra $100 this week? Not "I'll think about it" or "I'll see how the week goes." I mean a real decision, the kind you don't quietly renegotiate with yourself by Wednesday because you feel tired or uncomfortable.

Until you make that decision, nothing else in this book will help very much. You could read every chapter, learn twenty-five possible ways to make money, and still end up exactly where you started. The missing piece isn't more information. It's deciding to act on what you already know.

The practical part comes next. The how-to information, the real options, and the specific ways to reach that hundred dollars are all waiting in the chapters ahead. But none of those strategies can work until you deal with what has been happening in your own head.

Before you turn the page, I want you to do one thing.

Think about the story you've been telling yourself about why you haven't done this already. Write it down if you can. Name it plainly on paper, where it can no longer hide behind the noise and distractions of the rest of your day.

Then ask yourself honestly: Is this actually true, or does it only feel true because I've repeated it for so long?

Answering that question is your first move.

CHAPTER 2
YOU DON'T NEED A PLAN, YOU NEED A START

There is a particular kind of procrastination that doesn't look like procrastination at all.

It looks like research. It looks like preparation. It looks like responsibility.

It is spending three weeks reading about different ways to make extra money without trying any of them. It is buying a course and completing every module but never actually doing the thing the course was meant to prepare you for. It is having a notebook full of ideas, a browser full of open tabs, and a growing sense that you are almost ready to begin.

This is called productive procrastination, and it is one of the most effective ways the fear we talked about in Chapter 1 continues to hold you back without ever revealing itself as fear.

That's because planning feels like progress. It feels responsible, measured, and smart. Nobody can accuse you of being reckless when you are doing research. Nobody can call you impulsive when you are carefully weighing your options. And as long as you are still planning, you cannot fail, because you haven't actually started yet.

The plan becomes an escape hatch from the risk of trying. The longer you stay in planning mode, the easier it becomes to remain there.

2.1 THE MYTH OF THE PERFECT MOMENT

At the root of over-planning is a belief most people hold without ever examining it directly: the belief that there is a right time to start. A moment when everything will be aligned, when you will feel ready, when conditions will finally be favorable enough to justify taking the leap.

I want to tell you plainly: **that moment does not exist.**

Think about the last time you told yourself "I'll start once things calm down." Maybe it was after the holidays. Maybe it was once the kids went back to school, or once a busy stretch at work finally let up, or once you got through whatever specific thing was eating your time and energy that month. Did that calmer version of life actually show up? For most people, the honest answer is no, or it showed up for about a week before something else filled the space.

I think part of what makes the perfect moment so tempting is that it lets you feel like you're making progress without actually moving forward. Preparing is easier than acting. Imagining how it'll go is easier than finding out how it actually goes. So the perfect moment becomes a kind of holding pattern, somewhere comfortable to circle while convincing yourself you're getting closer, when really you're just burning fuel without ever taking off. From the outside, a year spent preparing looks almost exactly like a year spent standing still.

There's nothing wrong with wanting to feel ready. The problem is that readiness tends to show up after you start, not before. It is a feeling that develops along the way. You do not feel ready and then begin. You begin, and somewhere in the middle of it, you start to feel like you know what you're doing.

You've already proven this to yourself, probably more than once, in places you wouldn't normally think to look.

For example, nobody feels ready to bring home their first child. There's no book, class, or piece of advice that fully prepares anyone for being a parent. You figure it out anyway, in real time, because the baby is already here, and there's no waiting until you feel ready.

The same thing happens with a new job. Almost everyone spends the first few days wondering if they made a mistake. You don't know where anything is, you're second-guessing what you said in meetings, and it seems like everyone else knows exactly what they're doing. But give it a few months, and you're the one answering questions from the newest hire, handling things without thinking twice, wondering why the job ever felt so intimidating in the first place. None of that confidence existed before you started. It only showed up because you did.

The same thing is true of countless moments we rarely stop to think about. Moving to a new city where you don't know a single person. Going on a first date with no idea whether you'll have anything to talk about. Starting college. Giving a presentation you weren't sure you were ready to give. At the time, each of those moments feels uncertain, uncomfortable, bigger than you think you can handle. Then, almost without noticing, they become part of your life. The confidence didn't come first. It came because you lived through the experience.

Some moments, though, don't give you time to prepare; they just force you to adapt instantly. Your computer screen goes black an hour before a major deadline, or the software your company uses completely updates overnight without warning. Suddenly, the system you knew is gone, and you're staring at something totally unfamiliar with the clock ticking. You don't have the option to take a three-week course to get ready for it. You click around, you try different things, and you figure it out under pressure because the work has to get done. The confidence to use the new system doesn't come before you click, it comes because you had no choice but to start typing.

The truth is, people do things they don't feel ready for every single day. Not because they enjoy uncertainty or because they're naturally fearless, but because life keeps moving. The confidence, knowledge, and resilience they need don't show up beforehand. They grow out of taking the next step.

Making extra money works exactly the same way. There is no amount of research that will make your first attempt feel smooth and certain. The smoothness comes from doing it once, then twice, then enough times that the uncertainty fades and the confidence grows in its place. You cannot shortcut that process with more planning. You can only begin it by starting.

2.2 WHAT HAPPENS WHEN YOU WAIT ANOTHER WEEK

Waiting feels safe. It can even feel responsible. But every week you spend waiting for the right moment is another week you remain exactly as short as you were before. The bill that's due doesn't pause while you get ready, and the stress that follows you to the kitchen table doesn't take a break out of respect for your planning process.

There's also a strange thing that happens to a plan the longer you sit on it without taking action: it starts to grow. What begins as "sell a few things I don't use" turns into "figure out the best platform, take professional photos, research pricing, and create an entire system" before you've sold a single item.

The longer an idea sits untouched, the more it tends to expand into something bigger and more intimidating than it ever needed to be. Action keeps a plan small and manageable. Waiting gives it room to grow.

I've watched this happen with something as simple as a garage full of things someone meant to sell. At first, it's just, "I'll list a few things this weekend." A month passes, and now it has become, "I need to organize everything first, figure out what's worth selling, and maybe rent a storage unit while I sort through it." The job grows larger every week it sits there, not because the stuff has changed, but because waiting has made the whole thing feel more complicated than it ever needed to be.

There's another kind of math worth doing here, even if it's uncomfortable. If you need $100 this week and wait another week to start, you haven't simply delayed the result by seven days. You may now be even further behind. Another bill may have come due, another expense may have appeared, or the original shortfall may have grown. Waiting didn't keep the situation from getting worse. It gave it more time to do exactly that.

2.3 THE ONE-THING PRINCIPLE: PICK ONE

I remember one week when an unexpected car repair left me needing money I hadn't planned to spend. The bill wasn't something I could put off, but there also wasn't enough room in my regular budget to absorb it. I didn't need a long-term business idea. I needed to figure out how to bring in extra money quickly.

So I made a list of every realistic possibility I could think of. I could sell things around the house, pick up local odd jobs, drive people or deliver food around town, join paid research studies, watch pets or children, or freelance using skills I already had. If there was a legitimate way to earn extra cash, it went on the list.

Then I started narrowing it down. Some options didn't fit my schedule. Others required tools, qualifications, or setup I didn't have yet. A few simply weren't a good fit for my personality, and I was honest with myself about that instead of pretending otherwise.

Rather than getting stuck on everything I couldn't do, I kept returning to one simple question: what can I realistically do this week?

Little by little, the list grew shorter. Eventually, one option stood out as the best fit for where I was in my life at that moment. I wasn't choosing a permanent path or trying to identify the greatest money-making opportunity available. I was simply choosing one thing I could actually begin. That made all the difference.

I think a lot of people get stuck because they're trying to solve the wrong problem. They believe they need to find the best possible way to make extra money. They don't. They only need to find one doable way to make extra money this week. Those are two very different goals.

The right choice depends on your schedule, your skills, your personality, where you live, and what you already have available. There is no single answer that works for everyone. There are dozens of good options, and many of them could work if you chose one and gave it a real chance.

Later in this book, you'll see a wide range of ways to earn extra money. Don't make the mistake of thinking you need to try all of them. Use the same filtering process we just talked about: strip away the ones that don't fit your schedule or lifestyle, be honest about what you are actually willing to do, and leave yourself with a tight, manageable shortlist. From that list, choose one.

Not necessarily the one with the highest earning potential or the one everyone else seems to be talking about. Choose the one you can realistically start.

There is something powerful about choosing one direction and giving it your full attention. Instead of spending the week bouncing between five different ideas, you can make real progress on one. Even if it doesn't turn out to be the perfect choice, you will learn something. You may earn something. Most importantly, you will prove to yourself that you can take an idea and turn it into action.

You can always choose a different path later. But you have to start walking before you can find out where a path might lead.

2.4 DONE IS BETTER THAN PERFECT

A quick warning before we go any further: perfectionism is going to show up. It won't announce itself as fear. It will sound like quality control, like wanting to do things the right way, or like needing just a little more time to prepare before you commit.

What perfectionism is really doing is quietly replacing the actual goal with a safer one. The real goal is to make $100 this week. The safer goal is to create a flawless plan, find the perfect approach, and do it in a way you would feel proud to explain to someone else. That can feel productive, but it rarely produces a result. There is always one more detail to improve, which means there is always another reason to delay.

The shift this chapter is asking you to make is simple: choose one thing and allow yourself to do it imperfectly. Not carelessly or recklessly. Just imperfectly, in the ordinary way almost everything is when you are doing it for the first time, working within real constraints, or moving forward before you have every detail figured out. Something done imperfectly will always take you further than something perfect that never leaves your head.

Perfectionism often shows up in ways that seem harmless. You rewrite a marketplace listing over and over because the description still doesn't sound quite right. You spend an hour comparing platforms instead of posting the item on the one you already use. You delay sending a message to a potential client because you want to make it sound more professional, or put off applying for a job because your résumé could still be improved. None of that hesitation necessarily leads to a better result. Most of the time, it simply postpones the moment when something could actually happen.

So carry this with you into the rest of the book: stop trying to start perfectly. Just start. The option you choose doesn't have to be the smartest one, the most polished one, or even the one you stick with long term. It only has to be doable enough for you to act on it.

You can improve something once it exists. You cannot improve something you never started.

2.5 MAKE THE DECISION FIRST

Here's what I want you to do before you turn the page: decide that you are going to make an extra $100 this week.

The chapters ahead will give you plenty of options for how to do it. Some will fit your life better than others, and you may not know yet which one you will choose. That's okay. The decision comes first.

Once you have truly decided on the result, the exact path becomes less important. You stop waiting for the perfect idea and start looking for something that will work. You become more willing to adjust, try another approach, and keep moving until you get there.

Without that decision, every option becomes something to debate. With it, every option becomes something to consider.

So don't commit to a perfect plan. Commit to the $100.

That is the assignment for this chapter: make the decision to act. Next, we need to redefine what success actually looks like so you don't accidentally trick yourself into thinking a solid start is a failure.

CHAPTER 3
REDEFINING WHAT SUCCESS LOOKS LIKE

By now, you've done some of the harder work. You've taken an honest look at what has been holding you back, and you've either decided or come very close to deciding that staying exactly where you are is no longer an option. That is real progress. Many people never get that far, not because they are incapable, but because they never stop long enough to recognize what is actually keeping them stuck.

Before we begin exploring the practical ways to earn money, there is one more thing we need to clear up: what success is supposed to look like. This matters because the target you set determines how you judge everything that comes next. If you expect one small step to solve your entire financial life, even real progress can feel disappointing. But if you understand that the goal is to earn an extra $100 this week, prove to yourself that you can make money outside of your regular paycheck, and learn what works for you, it becomes much easier to recognize progress when you see it.

If you are aiming at the wrong target, you can do everything right and still walk away feeling like you failed. If you are aiming at the right one, even a small result can become the beginning of something much bigger.

3.1 FORGET "FINANCIAL FREEDOM" AND JUST FOCUS ON THIS WEEK

Open almost any other book about earning extra money, and before long you'll come across the same handful of phrases: financial freedom, passive income, building wealth, escaping the nine-to-five. They've been repeated so often that they've started to lose their meaning, the way almost any phrase does once it has appeared on enough book covers.

There is nothing wrong with those goals. Some of them may even be possible for you eventually. But here's the problem with starting there: they describe a destination that can feel impossibly far away from where you are standing right now. If you're trying to figure out how to cover a bill due in three days, a conversation about building long-term wealth isn't particularly helpful. It can feel almost insulting. It's like being hungry today and being handed a five-year meal plan instead of something to eat.

This book is going to do something different. It isn't going to ask you to imagine some distant version of financial freedom and work backward from there. It is going to ask you to focus on something much smaller, much closer, and far more immediate: an extra $100 by the end of this week.

That is the entire goal for now.

Not because bigger goals aren't worthwhile, but because a goal you can act on today is more useful than one that still feels too far away to reach. **A big goal without a clear next step is often little more than a wish with better branding.**

There is a certain kind of relief that comes from shrinking the target this way. You do not have to solve your entire financial life this week. You do not need to figure out your five-year plan, your retirement strategy, or your path toward some distant version of freedom.

You only need to solve this week.

That is something you can actually finish. And right now, completing one clear, immediate goal is worth more than chasing something so distant and vague that it doesn't yet feel real.

It also helps to understand how differently these two kinds of goals work. A goal like financial freedom does not have a finish line you can point to on any given Tuesday. It is vague by nature, which makes it difficult to know whether you are succeeding, failing, or simply moving in the right direction. You can work toward it for years without ever reaching a moment when you can honestly say, "There. That's done."

Making an extra $100 this week is different. Either you reach that goal or you don't. That kind of clarity can feel uncomfortable because it leaves less room to hide behind vague progress. But that is also exactly what makes it useful.

A goal you can finish is a goal you can prove to yourself you are capable of reaching. Once you reach it, you have something real to build on.

3.2 WHY THE METHOD MATTERS LESS THAN YOU THINK

Here's something worth saying again, because it's easy to agree with it now and forget it the moment you start reading through the options later in this book: **the specific way you make that $100 matters far less than most people think.**

It's tempting to treat this like a research problem. You assume there must be one perfect option somewhere, the one with the highest hourly return, the least effort, or the fewest drawbacks, and that your job is to find it before you begin.

The reality is much simpler. Someone who has genuinely decided to make an extra $100 this week will usually find a way forward without first identifying the perfect opportunity. Three people with the same level of determination might take three completely different paths. One might sell things they no longer need. Another might pick up a few hours of local work. A third might find an option the others never would have considered. The paths may be different, but each one begins with the same decision to act.

That is also why I didn't begin this book by jumping straight into a long list of ideas and step-by-step instructions. Knowing what you could do is not the same as deciding what you will do. Without that decision, even the most practical advice can become one more thing you read, consider, and never use.

There is a real difference between wanting something and deciding to do it. You can want to start exercising and get in shape. You might even buy a gym membership, order new workout clothes, and spend hours researching the best routine. But none of that means you have truly committed. Commitment begins when you show up at the gym and follow through, even on the days when you don't feel motivated.

You can want to save more money, eat healthier, apply for a better job, or finally clean out the garage. You can think about those things for months and make plans that never turn into action. A decision is different. A decision changes what you do next.

The same is true here. You can want an extra $100. You can read every idea in this book, highlight the ones that sound promising, and tell yourself you will try something soon. But until you decide that you are going to earn that extra $100 this week, it is still just something you want.

The chapters ahead will show you many possible ways to reach that goal. The exact path is less important than your decision to keep moving until you find one that works. That is the difference I want you to recognize before we go any further.

Wanting leaves room to keep waiting. A decision changes what you do next.

3.3 $100 ISN'T THE GOAL. IT'S PROOF

If $100 sounds small to you, you're not wrong. Compared with most of the financial concerns people carry, it is a small amount. But that is exactly the point, and it's worth understanding why.

A hundred dollars earned this week through your own effort does something a much larger, hypothetical goal cannot do. It becomes real. It isn't a plan, a projection, or a number on a five-year chart that depends on a dozen things going right. It is earned. It is finished. And once you have accomplished something, it becomes evidence in a way that intentions never can.

This is where an idea from earlier in the book comes back around: a small goal you actually reach beats a huge goal that remains stuck in "someday." You cannot argue with a hundred dollars you actually earned. You can argue with a dream you haven't acted on yet, and many people quietly do that for years.

So when you reach $100 this week, don't measure it against your rent, your debt, or whatever larger number has been sitting in the back of your mind. Measure it against where you were one week ago, when earning extra money may have felt like something other people could do, but not something you had proven you could do yourself.

That is the comparison worth making. By that measure, $100 is not small at all. It confirms something that was once only a possibility.

And that creates momentum. When next week begins, you are no longer starting from the same place. You are starting with experience and the knowledge that you can take action and produce a result. You may choose the same approach again, or you may try something different. Either way, the next step becomes easier because you are no longer asking whether you are capable of doing this.

You already know that you are.

That knowledge may be worth more than the hundred dollars itself, even though earning the money is what gave it to you.

This is worth sitting with for a moment because it is easy to read past. Many people spend years wondering whether they are the kind of person who can earn extra money when they need to. They never truly answer the question because they never put themselves to the test. Instead, they continue collecting reasons to believe one version of the story or the other without doing anything that could settle it.

One completed week breaks that cycle in a way that years of uncertainty never could. You no longer have to wonder. You have an answer, something solid to build on, and momentum to carry into next week.

3.4 THIS ISN'T A BUSINESS. IT'S A BRIDGE.

It's worth being clear about what this book is not so you can set realistic expectations for what it can help you accomplish.

This is not a guide to building a business. It is not a blueprint for replacing your income, retiring early, or leaving your job entirely. Some of the ideas in these pages may eventually grow into something bigger, and if that happens for you, that's great. But that is not what this book is promising. Expecting the extra $100 you make this week to somehow become $10,000 a month by next year only sets you up to overlook what you actually accomplished.

Think of this book as a bridge instead. A bridge is not where you live, and it is not the final destination. It simply gets you from one side of a gap to the other. Sometimes you may need that bridge more than once. Other times, you may only need it to get through one difficult week before returning to your normal life. Both are perfectly valid reasons to use it.

That distinction changes what success looks like. If you expect to build a business, making $100 once and then stopping can feel like giving up. But if the goal is to create a bridge, making $100 and getting yourself back onto solid ground means it worked exactly as intended. You do not need to feel guilty for failing to build a company out of something that helped you through one tight week. That was never its purpose.

There is also a trap worth naming because it catches a lot of well-meaning people: the belief that if something works once, you are obligated to scale it, earn more from it, or keep doing it long after it has fulfilled its purpose.

You are not.

If something helps you make $100 this week and you are satisfied with that, you are allowed to stop there and move on. You are not required to turn it into a side hustle, a business, or a permanent part of your schedule simply because it worked.

The bridge did its job the moment it got you across.

3.5 WHAT CHANGES ONCE YOU'VE DONE IT ONCE

Something changes after you earn that first $100. It can be difficult to fully describe until you experience it, but it is worth naming now so you recognize it when it happens.

The stories from Chapter 1 start to get quieter. The voice that said you didn't have enough time has less to say because you found the time. The belief that you were too old to try something new becomes harder to defend because you tried it anyway. The fear that you lacked the skills or experience anyone would value begins to lose its grip because you found a way to create a real result with what you already had.

Those stories may not disappear completely. But they become much harder to believe.

Not because you argued with them or forced yourself to think more positively, but because you did the very thing they told you that you couldn't do. A story built on repetition has a difficult time surviving a clear piece of evidence to the contrary, and that first $100 becomes exactly that.

You will probably notice that the second time feels different too. There may be less dread beforehand and less of that knot in your stomach we talked about in Chapter 1, the one that appears whenever you are about to do something unfamiliar. That is not necessarily because the work itself has become easier. It is because you are no longer doing it for the first time. You now have proof that you can start, follow through, and get a result.

That proof changes the way you approach the opportunities in the chapters ahead. They stop feeling like theoretical ideas you have to analyze from every angle and start becoming real options you can choose from. You no longer have to search for the perfect answer. You can choose something that fits, try it imperfectly, and give it a real chance to work.

So as you move into the next chapters, keep the size and purpose of the goal in mind. You are not trying to achieve financial freedom this week. You are not trying to build a business. You are making an extra $100 and proving that the stories you once told yourself were never the whole truth.

Once you have that proof, the question changes. It is no longer whether you can do it. It is simply which bridge you will cross first.

CHAPTER 4
START WITH WHAT YOU HAVE

This is where the practical part of the book begins.

Everything up to this point has been about clearing the ground: looking honestly at what has been holding you back, deciding that this week is going to be different, and understanding what you are actually trying to accomplish. That work was not separate from what comes next. It is what makes action possible. But now it is time to move from thinking about making extra money to actually doing something about it.

The chapters ahead will give you practical options, specific examples, and a wide range of ways to bring in extra money. You will also find a list of 300 money-making ideas at the end of the book, so you can quickly scan for options that may work for you. Some will fit your life better than others. **If you're unsure where to begin, start here: with what you already have**.

It really is the easiest place to start because you don't need to find anything new, learn a new skill, or wait for an opportunity to appear. You simply need to take a closer look at what is already yours.

4.1 THE MONEY HIDING IN PLAIN SIGHT

Almost everyone has more sellable items sitting around than they realize. We stop noticing things once they become part of the background of our homes. The exercise bike that turned into a clothes rack. The monitor left over from an upgraded computer setup. The small kitchen appliance that has been sitting untouched in a cabinet for two years. After a while, these things stop feeling like possessions with value. They simply become part of the room.

That is exactly why this is such a good place to start. You are not creating value from nothing or learning how to do something new. The value is already sitting in your home, doing nothing for you, while someone nearby may be willing to pay for it.

Start by making this as easy as possible. Look for a few things you no longer use, would not miss, and could realistically sell for around $100 each. You are not committing to selling all of them. You are giving yourself several strong possibilities so you are not depending on one item to attract the right buyer immediately.

Begin with the higher-value items because one sale could be enough to reach your entire goal. Look for unused furniture, electronics, exercise equipment, tools, musical instruments, lawn equipment, gaming systems, appliances, collectibles, or anything else that still has meaningful resale value. Focus on the things that have been sitting untouched for months or years, especially anything you replaced, upgraded, or stopped using.

The question to ask is not, "Do I still like this?" or "Could I possibly use this again someday?" Ask yourself, "Would I genuinely miss this if it were gone?" If the honest answer is no, it may be worth more to you as cash than it is sitting in a closet, basement, garage, or spare room.

If you genuinely cannot find five items that might sell for at least \$100, widen the search. Look for things that could bring in between \$50 and \$100. Two smaller sales can get you to the same goal just as effectively as one larger sale. The point is not to find the most impressive item in your house. It is to identify the shortest, simplest path to the \$100 you need.

This may feel harder than it should because we develop a strange attachment to things simply because we have owned them for a long time. Even an item we rarely notice can suddenly feel important when we think about letting it go. Often, though, the resistance is not really about the item. It is about the fears that surface when we consider selling it. *What if I need it someday? What if I regret letting it go? What if someone I know sees the listing and wonders why I am selling my things?* These worries can make an ordinary decision feel far more significant than it really is.

Most of those fears are about possibilities, not realities. You might need the item someday, but you have not needed it in months or even years. And if you truly do need another kitchen appliance or household item later, you can always buy one when that need actually arises. Someone you know might see the listing, but they are unlikely to think much about it, and there is nothing embarrassing about selling something you no longer use. You do not have to get rid of anything meaningful or difficult to replace. The goal is simply to look honestly at what is sitting unused and decide whether keeping it is more valuable than turning it into money you can use right now.

4.2 WHAT ACTUALLY SELLS (AND WHAT DOESN'T)

It helps to have a general sense of what tends to sell quickly and what may sit for a while, so you know what to expect. This is not a complete list or a set of hard rules. It is simply a rough guide to the kinds of items that usually attract buyers faster than others.

Items that sell quickly are often practical things people use regularly but do not want to buy at full retail price. Furniture in decent condition can do well, especially basic pieces that work in many different homes. Exercise equipment may also move quickly, partly because so many people buy it with enthusiasm and then quietly stop using it. Working electronics, even older models, often still have value. The same can be true for tools, children's gear that is only needed for a short stage of life, and seasonal items listed shortly before people are likely to need them.

Items that sit longer are often highly personal or specific to one person's taste. Artwork and home decor can take time because the right buyer has to like that particular style. Broken items, including those described as "probably fixable," may also struggle to attract interest because buyers often assume they will require more time and effort than they are worth. Listings can also sit when the price is based on what the seller originally paid rather than what the item is realistically worth now.

Clothing and books deserve a separate mention because they do not fit neatly into either category. With these items, success often depends less on finding one individual buyer and more on choosing the right place to sell them. A general listing for a bag of clothes may not attract much attention, but a consignment or secondhand store that specializes in that type of clothing may take several pieces at once, especially recognizable brands in good condition.

Books can work the same way through a different outlet. I have sold sizable stacks of books through websites that buy them in bulk, provide a price upfront, and have you ship the entire box rather than list each title separately. The amount you receive for each individual piece of clothing or book is usually small, but it can add up when you have a large quantity. It is also a practical way to declutter your home while making some money from things that might otherwise continue taking up space.

Jewelry is another category worth checking, especially pieces made from gold, silver, or other valuable materials. Depending on the type and value of the piece, you might consider a local jewelry store, gold buyer, pawn shop, consignment store, or online resale platform. Even broken or outdated jewelry may be worth something because of its metal content, so do not assume it has no value simply because you no longer wear it.

None of this is a guarantee. Unusual items sell every day, while supposedly easy items may sit if they are priced too high, poorly photographed, or listed in the wrong place. Still, having a general sense of what tends to move can keep you from becoming discouraged if your first item does not sell immediately.

4.3 CHOOSE WHERE TO SELL IT

There are more places to sell things than most people realize, but you do not need to use all of them. Just start with one that makes sense for what you are selling and feels comfortable for you to use.

A good way to decide where to list something is to think about how you would buy it yourself. If you were looking for a used coffee table, lawn mower, or exercise bike, where would you search first? If you wanted a collectible, a specific electronic device, or a hard-to-find replacement part, where would you expect to find it? The easier it is for the right buyer to come across your item, the better your chances of selling it.

It also helps to start with a platform you already understand. If you have bought something through Facebook Marketplace, Craigslist, a local resale group, or another site, you already have a general sense of how the listings work, how buyers communicate, and what the process looks like. There is no reason to make your first sale harder by learning an entirely new platform unless the item clearly belongs somewhere else.

If you are unsure where to begin and already use Facebook, Facebook Marketplace or a local buy-sell-trade group can be a good place to start. Both can help you reach nearby buyers, avoid shipping, and sell common household items such as furniture, appliances, exercise equipment, tools, electronics, and children's gear. You may also be able to share a Marketplace listing with one or more local groups, giving the item more visibility without starting from scratch. You will probably hear from some people who never follow through, but the familiar setup and access to local buyers can still make Facebook one of the easier places to begin.

Craigslist may feel dated, but it can still be useful for large or bulky items that are difficult or expensive to ship. It is free, local, and fairly simple to use. It is also one of my favorite places to sell things. I have used it to sell a bike, a computer monitor, a Keurig coffee maker, kitchen items, and sports equipment. Because there is very little buyer verification or built-in protection, you should use extra caution when arranging payment and pickup.

Selling directly to friends, relatives, coworkers, or neighbors is easy to overlook because it may not feel like a formal sale. But it can be one of the fastest and simplest options. You do not even have to ask someone directly whether they want to buy the item. You can simply ask whether they know anyone who might be interested, which can take some of the pressure out of approaching people you know. A short text message or a post on your personal Facebook page may be enough to find a buyer without creating a public listing, answering questions from strangers, or arranging several meetups. It will not work for every item, but it may be worth trying before you list something publicly.

A traditional garage sale can make sense if you have a large number of things to sell at once. It works especially well for smaller, lower-value items that may not be worth photographing and listing individually. A garage sale does take some time to organize, price your items, set everything up, and advertise the sale beforehand. You may not receive the highest possible price for every item, but you can clear out a significant amount in a single morning and avoid managing dozens of separate listings.

A pawn shop may be worth considering if you need money quickly and do not want to wait for an individual buyer. Pawn shops commonly purchase jewelry, tools, electronics, musical instruments, and collectibles, and you may be able to leave with cash the same day. The tradeoff is that you will usually receive less than you might through a private sale, so this option is better for speed and convenience than for getting the highest possible price.

eBay and, in some cases, Amazon, are also options, but both take more time and effort to set up than local selling platforms. eBay works well for collectibles, niche electronics, discontinued items, and anything that may need a larger pool of buyers. Amazon is generally better suited to new or unused products and people who plan to continue selling. Both can be useful, but they are probably not the easiest places to begin if your goal is simply to make an extra $100.

The most important thing is not choosing the platform with the most features or the largest possible audience. It is choosing a place where someone is likely to look for your item and where you feel comfortable selling it. Think about where you would search for the item yourself, choose the easiest reasonable option, and list it there. You can always try another place later if it does not sell.

4.4 LEARNING JUST ENOUGH TO GET STARTED

Here is where the done-is-better-than-perfect mindset from earlier in the book becomes especially useful. You will need to learn a few small, practical things: how to create a listing, how to take clear photos, and what information buyers expect to see. Spending a little time learning those basics is completely reasonable.

What you do not need to do is turn that preparation into another excuse to delay. You do not need to watch an hour of videos about professional product photography before listing a used coffee maker, or study pricing psychology before posting an exercise bike no one in your house has touched in a year. Spend a few minutes looking at similar listings to understand the basic format and get a sense of a reasonable price. You can also ask yourself what you would honestly be willing to pay for the item if you were the buyer. That is usually enough information to create the listing and put it online.

The process is also easier than it has ever been. You can use an AI tool like ChatGPT to help you turn the basic details about an item into a clear, honest description. You can also ask it for general instructions if you are unsure how a particular website or app works.

That can save you time, but always review the result carefully before using it. Make sure the description accurately reflects the item's condition, features, size, brand, and any flaws. Do not let ChatGPT embellish the details, make unsupported claims, or describe the item as being in better condition than it really is. You should also confirm any specific information about fees, policies, or platform requirements on the actual site. Those details can change, and taking a minute to verify them is better than relying on instructions that may be outdated.

The best approach is to get one listing posted, even if it is not perfect, and learn the rest as you go. Once the item is live, you will probably learn more from seeing how buyers respond than you would from spending another hour researching beforehand. Maybe your price is a little high and you lower it. Maybe the photo needs better lighting and you replace it. Those things are easy to fix after the listing is posted. None of them is a reason to delay putting it up in the first place.

You can improve the listing later. First, you have to post it.

4.5 LOOK AT WHAT YOU OWN DIFFERENTLY

Even after you identify something worth selling and choose where to list it, another obstacle may show up: embarrassment.

You may feel awkward about people knowing you are selling your belongings. You may worry that someone will assume you are struggling financially or wonder why you need the money. You might feel uncomfortable posting an item where friends, neighbors, or coworkers could see it.

But think about the situation from the buyer's side.

How would you feel if you found a gently used item you needed at a reasonable price? You probably would not think less of the person selling it. You would be happy that you found a good deal and relieved that you did not have to pay full price for something that still had plenty of use left in it.

There is nothing awkward about buying a used piece of furniture, an appliance, a bike, a computer monitor, a piece of sports equipment, or almost anything else. It is a normal transaction.

The buyer gets something useful at a fair price, and the seller gets money for something they no longer need.

So why should it feel any different when you are the one selling?

In many cases, selling an item is also better than allowing it to sit unused for years or eventually throwing it away. Someone else gets to use it, you clear space in your home, and you put money back into your pocket.

But you do not necessarily have to give something up permanently to make money from it. Selling is only one way to benefit from what you already own. In some cases, renting it may make more sense.

You may be able to rent out a spare room, a garage, a parking space, a vehicle, tools, equipment, storage space, or something else that spends most of its time sitting empty. A driveway near a stadium or event venue could become paid parking on busy days. A tool sitting untouched in your garage might be exactly what someone nearby needs for one afternoon.

There are platforms that help connect people who have unused space, vehicles, or equipment with people who need temporary access to them. My brother actually rented out his van. Instead of leaving it parked and unused, he allowed someone else to use it and made money from something he already owned. He did not need to create a product, learn a specialized skill, or build a business. He simply recognized that something sitting in his driveway had value to someone else.

Of course, renting something requires more thought than selling it. You need to consider insurance, liability, local rules, platform requirements, possible damage, and whether you are genuinely comfortable allowing someone else to use the item or space. Those details are important, and you should confirm them before agreeing to anything.

That is really the larger point of this chapter. There are far more ways to make money from what you already own than most people ever stop to consider. Selling something on a marketplace is the obvious option, so it is the one people talk about most. But renting unused belongings or space can create possibilities you may not have considered before.

The real question is not simply, *What can I sell?* It is broader than that: *What do I already have, and how could I use it to make extra money?* You might sell it. You might rent it. You might discover another possibility that had never occurred to you before. Once you take an honest look at what you own, you may realize that the value was there all along.

The things sitting quietly in the background of your life may have more earning potential than you realize. You just have to start seeing them through the eyes of someone who might value them.

CHAPTER 5
EASY SHORT-TERM MONEY

The previous chapter was about making money from what you already own. This one is about something different: what you can do with your time and the skills you already have.

These options often receive less attention because they are not usually presented as part of a business plan or a path to financial freedom. They may not sound impressive or involve a clever strategy. Most simply require you to show up and do something another person needs done. But that simplicity is exactly what makes them useful when you need money quickly.

Unlike selling something you own, these opportunities can often be repeated. You can babysit again, take another cleaning job, or donate plasma again when you are eligible. You do not need to turn any of them into a business or make them part of a long-term plan. They are simply practical ways to earn money when you need it.

Most of the ideas in this chapter do not require specialized training. They require reliability, a willingness to do the work, and sometimes a willingness to take on tasks that may not feel impressive or glamorous.

5.1 GETTING PAID JUST FOR BEING AVAILABLE (AND WILLING): PLASMA DONATION AND PAID STUDIES

One of the more overlooked ways to make quick money is simply by participating in something rather than using a skill or completing a task. Plasma donation is probably the most familiar example. Donation centers compensate eligible donors for their time, often allowing more than one visit per week. The amount varies by location, center, and current promotions.

Not everyone will qualify to donate plasma, and even if you do, you may decide the experience is not worth it for you. The process can take an hour or two, especially during your first visit when there is additional screening and paperwork. There is also a needle involved, along with blood and the possibility that you may feel tired or lightheaded afterward. If you dislike needles or blood, or simply do not have one or two hours available for each visit, skip this option.

I tried plasma donation myself. I did not love it, but during the initial promotional period, I earned about $700 in one month. That money paid for new tires for my car, which made it worth it. Once the promotional period ended, I chose not to continue.

Paid research studies are a less commonly discussed version of the same idea. Universities, hospitals, medical centers, and private research companies regularly pay people to participate. Some require only a short online session or a single appointment, while others involve more extensive testing, multiple visits, or a longer commitment.

I have participated in numerous research studies and have been paid anywhere from about $50 to $500 per study, depending on what was involved and how much time it required. I have completed questionnaires, tested apps, had MRIs, given blood, and taken part in other types of research.

You will also need to qualify. Researchers may be looking for people of a certain age, health status, background, or lifestyle, depending on what they are studying. You may apply for several opportunities before finding one that fits. Read the details carefully, ask questions if anything is unclear, and make sure you understand when and how you will be paid.

If you live near a university, paid studies may be an especially good option. Universities often recruit participants through psychology departments, medical schools, business programs, and other research centers. You can search the university's website for participant opportunities or look online for paid studies in your area.

Plasma donation and paid studies share the same basic idea: you are being paid for your time and willingness to participate. Neither option is right for everyone, but if you are eligible and comfortable with what is required, they can be relatively easy ways to make some extra cash.

5.2 WATCHING KIDS, PETS, AND HOMES

Babysitting, pet sitting, dog walking, and house sitting are some of the oldest ways to make extra money, and they are still good options for a reason. People regularly need someone dependable to watch their children, care for their pets, or check on their homes while they are away. Because these jobs are built around trust, the people who already know you may be the best place to begin.

Watching kids can be a good option, especially if families in your neighborhood or social circle already know and trust you. Parents may need someone for an occasional evening out, a few hours after school, or regular help during weekends or school breaks. Even one or two babysitting jobs could bring you much closer to your $100 goal.

Caregiving platforms such as Care.com can connect babysitters and other caregivers with families seeking support, but creating a profile does not guarantee immediate work. Families may compare several people, conduct interviews, request references, review qualifications, or require a background check before choosing someone. The platform can be useful if you want to find ongoing work, but reaching out to people you already know may be the faster place to begin.

You do not need to be a professional nanny or an expert babysitter, but you should genuinely like being around children, be patient and responsible, and know how to respond to a basic emergency. First aid and CPR certifications are valuable qualifications and may help parents feel more comfortable trusting you with their children. You should also be honest about the ages and number of children you can safely manage. Watching one independent ten-year-old is very different from caring for an infant and two toddlers.

Many of the same principles apply to pet care. People need someone they can trust to walk their dogs, feed their cats, provide company while they are at work, or care for their animals while they travel. Pet care platforms such as Rover can connect you with people in your area who need dog walking, drop-in visits, overnight care, or someone to keep a pet in their home.

These platforms make it easier to find customers outside your existing circle, and their profiles, reviews, and messaging systems can help establish trust before a job begins. The downside is that getting your first customer may take time. When you are new to a platform, you do not have reviews, repeat clients, or a history that helps people feel confident choosing you. You may need to create a strong profile, set a competitive starting price, respond quickly to requests, and wait for someone to give you that first opportunity. The platform may also take a portion of what you earn. It can still be worth setting up, but it may not be the fastest route if you need $100 within the next few days.

Once again, your own network may get you there faster. Think about the people you already know and the problems they are already paying someone else to solve. Maybe your neighbor takes her dog to an expensive doggie daycare several days a week, while you work from home and would be happy to watch the dog during the day. You could charge less than the daycare, save your neighbor money, and still earn a worthwhile amount for something that fits naturally into your schedule.

Before offering to watch a dog in your home, make sure your living situation is appropriate for it. Consider whether you have enough space, whether your yard is secure, and whether your lease or homeowners association allows it. If you have pets of your own, you also need to know how they respond to other animals. Most importantly, make sure everyone else who lives in the house is comfortable with the arrangement. Bringing someone else's dog into your home affects them too.

Pet sitting does not always mean having an animal stay with you. Sometimes people simply need someone to stop by while they are on vacation, feed the cats, refresh their water, scoop the litter box, and make sure everything looks normal. Others may need someone to walk the dog, give medication, or spend time with a pet that does not do well alone. These smaller jobs can be easier to fit into your schedule than full-day or overnight care.

Loving animals is a good start, but it is not the only requirement. You should be comfortable following feeding schedules, handling leashes safely, cleaning up accidents, and recognizing when something may be wrong. A calm older dog may be easy for you to watch, while a large, reactive dog may be far beyond what you can safely handle. Know your limits and do not accept a job simply because you need the money.

House sitting is another option built around dependability, although the responsibilities are usually different. Someone who is traveling may need a person to bring in the mail, water plants, take out the trash, check the property, or make the home look occupied. Some homeowners only need a quick visit every day or two. Others may want someone to stay overnight, especially if pets are involved or they will be gone for an extended period.

Before accepting any of these jobs, make sure both sides understand exactly what is included. How many hours will you be responsible for the child, pet, or home? Are overnight stays required? Will you need to drive anywhere, give medication, prepare meals, clean up, or complete other household tasks? Confirm the payment, schedule, emergency contacts, and expectations before the job begins. What sounds like a simple favor can quickly become much more work when the details are left unclear.

Watching children, caring for pets, and looking after homes all depend largely on trust. That can make it harder to get started with complete strangers, but it also makes your existing relationships especially valuable. Someone who already knows that you are dependable may be much more willing to hire you or recommend you to someone else. The quickest opportunity may not be waiting on an app. It may belong to someone you already know.

But if you do not know anyone who needs these services, or you do not feel comfortable reaching out to people in your personal life, there are plenty of other ways to find opportunities. Caregiving and pet care platforms, neighborhood groups, community bulletin boards, and local social media pages can help connect you with people who are actively looking for help. It may take a little longer to establish trust with someone new, but a clear profile, references, and reliable communication can help you get started.

5.3 CLEANING, ORGANIZING, AND THE JOBS PEOPLE WANT OFF THEIR PLATE

There is a wide category of work that exists simply because people would rather pay someone else than do it themselves, especially when they are busy or need help on short notice. Cleaning a house before guests arrive, organizing a garage or closet that has gotten out of hand, helping someone pack or unpack during a move, or catching up on yard work after a busy season can all become opportunities to make extra money.

TaskRabbit is one of the better-known platforms for this kind of work. Getting started involves creating a profile, choosing which services you want to offer, setting your rate, and completing a background check. The platform adds fees to the amount the customer pays, so you need to keep the final price in mind when setting a competitive rate. As with most platforms, there is also some setup involved, and it may take time to get your first job when you do not yet have reviews.

TaskRabbit is only one option. There are many other platforms where you can list your services, depending on the type of work you want to do. Some focus on cleaning, moving help, yard work, handyman services, or other household tasks, while more general freelance and local service platforms allow you to advertise several different kinds of help. Search for the specific service you want to offer along with the name of your city to see which platforms are active in your area.

You can also look for people who are already hiring. Craigslist, local job boards, community groups, and traditional job platforms sometimes have listings for cleaners, organizers, movers, event workers, and other short-term help. I once found a job cleaning Airbnbs through Craigslist. It was not an opportunity I would have known existed if I had only looked at platforms designed specifically for household tasks.

But you do not need an app or job listing to find this kind of work. In fact, your own network may be the faster place to start. People mention these problems all the time without realizing that someone they know might be willing to help. A friend may be overwhelmed before a move. A neighbor may be dreading cleaning before family arrives. Someone may need help organizing a basement, carrying furniture, or finally dealing with a yard that has been neglected for weeks.

The problem is that they may not know you are available, and you may not realize they would gladly pay for help.

A short, low-pressure message or social media post can change that. Let friends, relatives, neighbors, and coworkers know that you are looking to pick up some extra work and are available for cleaning, organizing, packing, yard work, or other household tasks. You do not need to explain your financial situation or make a formal sales pitch. You are simply letting people know that you are available if they, or someone they know, could use the help.

Even when the person you contact does not need help, they may know someone who does. A friend might have a neighbor preparing to move, a coworker might know someone looking for a cleaner, or a relative might hear that someone needs help clearing out a garage. Word-of-mouth recommendations are especially valuable for this kind of work because people are more comfortable hiring someone who has been recommended by a person they trust.

That is one reason your network can produce results faster than a platform. You do not need to wait for someone to discover your profile or take a chance on a person with no reviews. Even a message sent to five people can travel much farther if each of them mentions your name to someone else.

That does not mean platforms and job listings are not worth using. You can create a profile, search existing listings, and reach out to people you know at the same time. Sending a few messages takes only minutes and may lead to work before you have even finished setting up an account or applying elsewhere.

Before accepting a job, make sure you understand exactly what the person expects. "Help me organize my garage" could mean sorting a few boxes or spending an entire day lifting heavy items and hauling away trash. "Clean the kitchen" could mean wiping down the counters or deep-cleaning every cabinet and appliance. Ask what needs to be done, how long they expect it to take, whether supplies or equipment will be provided, and how much you will be paid before you agree.

You should also be honest about what you are willing and physically able to do. You do not need to be a professional cleaner or organizer, but you should be dependable and capable of completing the work you accept. If you cannot safely lift heavy furniture, operate certain equipment, climb ladders, or work outdoors in extreme weather, do not agree to it simply because you need the money. There will be other tasks that fit you better.

There is no shortage of people who need help getting things done. The challenge is making sure they know you are available. List your services, check local job postings, and tell the people in your network what kind of work you are willing to take on. One cleaning job, moving project, or afternoon of yard work may be enough to put the extra money you need in your pocket.

5.4 USE THE SKILLS YOU ALREADY HAVE

You may have skills that feel so ordinary to you that you have never considered charging for them. Maybe you are good at setting up technology, baking, styling hair, assembling furniture, organizing paperwork, taking photographs, or helping someone prepare for a job interview. Because these things come naturally to you, it is easy to assume they would not be valuable to anyone else.

But something does not have to be difficult for you to be useful to someone else.

The person struggling to connect a printer may gladly pay someone who can get it working in twenty minutes. Someone applying for jobs may want help proofreading a résumé or completing an online application. A neighbor hosting a birthday party may be happy to pay someone else to make cupcakes, take photographs, decorate, or help set everything up.

The goal here is not to turn your skill into a full freelance career. It is to find one person with one immediate problem you already know how to solve.

Start by thinking about what people already ask you to help with. Are you the person relatives call when they cannot figure out their phones? Do friends ask you to proofread important messages, wrap gifts, style their hair, create invitations, decorate cakes, or help them get organized? Those requests may point directly to something another person would pay you to do.

Your previous jobs and everyday experience can also give you useful skills. If you have worked in an office, you may be able to help someone organize files, enter information into a spreadsheet, prepare documents, or sort through paperwork. Restaurant experience could make you useful when someone needs help preparing food for a party. Retail experience may help you price items for a garage sale, organize inventory, or set up a display for a small event.

The best offers are specific. "I can help with computers" is vague. "I can set up your new phone, connect your printer, transfer your photos, or show you how to use basic apps" gives people a much clearer reason to hire you. Instead of simply saying you can bake, mention that you can make cookies or cupcakes for a small event. Instead of saying you are good at writing, offer to proofread a résumé, cover letter, school paper, or important document.

Specific offers help people immediately recognize a problem you can solve.

Let friends, relatives, neighbors, coworkers, and social media contacts know what you are available to do. Since this chapter is about making money relatively quickly, start with the people who already know and trust you rather than spending days building a professional profile. Even if the person you contact does not need your help, they may know someone who does.

Before agreeing to anything, make sure you understand what the person expects and how much work is involved. "Help with my résumé" could mean fixing a few sentences or rewriting the entire document. "Take pictures at my party" could mean thirty minutes of casual photographs or several hours of work followed by editing. Confirm what you will do, when it needs to be finished, and how much you will be paid before you begin.

You should also be honest about what you can do safely and competently. You do not need to be the leading expert, but you should be capable of delivering what you promise. Some services may also require a license, certification, permit, insurance, or compliance with local rules, particularly when food, beauty services, home repairs, health, or safety are involved. Check before accepting paid work if you are unsure.

The skill most likely to make you money this week may not be your most impressive one. It may simply be the one that solves a clear problem for someone right now. A few hours setting up technology, proofreading documents, preparing food, or helping with an event could be enough to bring in the extra money you need.

5.5 WHY "BENEATH YOU" ISN'T A REAL CATEGORY

There is a quiet discomfort some people may feel about the options in this chapter, even if they never say it out loud. Babysitting, cleaning houses, or donating plasma can feel like lesser ways to make money, the kind of things you do only when you have no other choice. Along with that can come a small worry about what taking on this kind of work might say about you.

That discomfort is worth examining because it is exactly the kind of story we talked about in Chapter 1, the kind that feels like a fact but is really just an idea you absorbed somewhere along the way. Nobody who hires a babysitter is judging the babysitter's life choices. Nobody who hires a cleaner thinks less of the person doing the work. They are grateful because they needed help with something they could not do, did not have time to do, or simply preferred to pay someone else to handle. The exchange is straightforward and useful to both people.

It is worth asking where the discomfort comes from. For many people, it is tied to an inherited idea about which kinds of work carry status and which do not. But status has very little to do with whether the work is honest, useful, or fairly paid. An hour of work that puts money in your pocket is not worth less because it does not come with an impressive title.

In fact, it may be worth asking whether the need to maintain a certain image has contributed to the financial pressure you are feeling now. Keeping up appearances can be expensive. Buying things you cannot comfortably afford, refusing work because it does not seem impressive enough, or pretending everything is fine when it is not can quietly make a difficult situation worse. Sometimes the smartest financial decision is the one that looks least impressive from the outside.

It is also important to remember that none of the ideas in this chapter are things you are being forced to do. They are simply options, relatively straightforward ways to make extra money when one of them fits your circumstances. You can choose the ones you are comfortable with and ignore the rest.

So if "that is beneath me" is the thought keeping you from considering these possibilities, treat it the same way you would any other story from Chapter 1. Notice it, question whether it is actually true, and decide whether it deserves to make the choice for you.

CHAPTER 6
STEADY WORK THAT ADDS UP

So far, we have focused mostly on ways to earn extra money quickly, whether that meant selling something you already owned or using a few hours of your time to complete a specific task. This chapter is a little different. The opportunities here may take longer to get started and often require more of an ongoing time commitment, but once they are in place, they can continue putting money in your pocket week after week.

Many of these options require an application, background check, interview, or simply some time spent finding the right fit. You may not be approved or selected for every opportunity you pursue, and the money may not arrive immediately. Still, getting started now could put you in a much better position next week and the week after that.

Some options let you choose your own hours, while others require regular shifts or recurring appointments. You can apply to a delivery app, respond to part-time job listings, and create a freelance profile all in the same week. Putting several opportunities in motion keeps your progress from depending on a single response.

6.1 GIG APPS: DRIVING AND DELIVERING

This is probably what most people think of first when they hear "gig work," and for good reason. Driving passengers through Uber or Lyft is one version. Food delivery through DoorDash, Uber Eats, or Grubhub is another. Grocery and household deliveries are available through apps such as Instacart, while Amazon Flex contracts independent drivers to deliver packages during scheduled blocks.

Depending on where you live, you may not even need a car. Some cities allow couriers to make food deliveries by bicycle or scooter, which eliminates many of the expenses that come with driving. These are only some of the better-known options, so check which services operate where you live.

One of the biggest advantages of gig apps is flexibility. You can generally choose when you work and decide how much or how little you want to do. You might drive for a few hours on a busy Friday night, make deliveries during the lunch rush, or work several long days when you need more money. That flexibility can make gig work easier to fit around another job, school, family responsibilities, or an unpredictable schedule.

When I lost my job, I started driving for Lyft. At first, I was terrified. Letting a stranger into my car felt uncomfortable, and I worried about getting lost, making a mistake, or not knowing how the app worked. But once I completed that first ride, the fear started to fade.

The more I drove, the more I learned. I figured out that I could earn more by driving during peak hours, paying attention to bonuses, and noticing which areas tended to be busiest. Eventually, I added Uber so I could use both apps instead of depending on only one. When Lyft was slow, I could check Uber, and when Uber was slow, I could switch back.

During my busiest weeks, I made between $700 and $1,000, but I worked a lot of hours to get there. The money was real, and it helped when I needed it. But the costs were real, too. Over time, the wear and tear on my car became too much.

If you plan to drive passengers or make deliveries by car, you need a reliable vehicle that meets the platform's requirements and can handle the additional mileage. Even a dependable car will need more frequent maintenance when you are adding hundreds of miles each week. Gas, oil changes, tires, repairs, insurance, tolls, and the gradual loss of value to the vehicle all reduce what you truly earn.

Pay also varies depending on where and when you work. A slow Tuesday afternoon may look nothing like a busy Friday night. Meal times, weekends, holidays, concerts, sporting events, weather, and local demand can all affect how much work is available. People who earn consistently usually learn which hours and locations are most profitable instead of simply turning on an app at random.

Using more than one platform can reduce downtime. You might drive for both Uber and Lyft or combine passenger rides with food delivery. Just do not let multiple apps distract you while driving or tempt you to accept work you cannot complete safely.

Each platform has its own application and approval process. You may need to provide identification, a valid driver's license, proof of insurance, vehicle information, and permission for a background check. Approval can take several days or longer, and some platforms may place new applicants on a waitlist depending on demand in your area.

Once you are approved, expect a learning curve. Your first few shifts will likely involve figuring out where to wait, which requests are worth accepting, and how to complete trips as efficiently as possible. As you gain experience, you'll develop strategies that help you earn more while wasting less time.

Another advantage of many gig apps is that they let you access your earnings quickly, sometimes on the same day. Although instant transfers often come with a small fee, they can be helpful when you need money right away.

Gig work is not perfect, and it is not free money. Your actual earnings depend on the hours you work, the demand in your area, and the expenses that come with the job. But if you have a reliable vehicle, enjoy a flexible schedule, and are willing to learn how the platforms work, driving and delivery apps can become a dependable way to bring in extra income whenever you need it.

6.2 FREELANCING, TUTORING, AND TEACHING

Freelancing, tutoring, and teaching are all ways to earn money by offering a defined service. Instead of picking up random tasks, you are using something you already know how to do and turning it into paid work that clients or students may need more than once.

This can include writing, editing, design, bookkeeping, photography, virtual assistance, social media support, translation, academic tutoring, music lessons, and many other services. Skilled work can often pay more per hour than driving or delivering, and a few regular clients or students can create more consistent income.

The tradeoff is that it usually takes longer to get started, and the work is not always predictable at first. You may need time to find clients, build trust, create samples, respond to messages, adjust your pricing, and prove that you can deliver what you promise.

Freelance platforms such as Fiverr and Upwork can be good options if you are willing to put in the work required to attract customers. You may need a strong profile, work samples, competitive pricing, proposals, and some form of promotion before orders begin coming in. Competition can be high, especially when you are new and do not have reviews or a marketing budget.

I have a Fiverr account where I offer book formatting services. It gives me a place to advertise something I already know how to do, but creating the listing did not automatically bring in customers. It takes time to get noticed, the platform takes a percentage of each sale, and there is a delay between completing an order and being able to withdraw the money.

Freelance marketplaces are not the only option. Teaching and tutoring have their own platforms. Preply and italki connect language tutors with students, while Cambly, Cambly Kids, and VIPKid offer opportunities to teach English. Outschool covers a wider range of subjects for children and teenagers. Other tutoring and teaching platforms may also be available depending on your subject, experience, and location. New platforms and opportunities continue to appear, so it is worth spending a few minutes searching online to see what is currently available for the skills you have to offer.

Whether you are freelancing, tutoring, or teaching, be specific about what you offer. "I do freelance work" is too broad. "I format paperback and ebook manuscripts," "I provide bookkeeping support for small businesses," or "I tutor middle school students in math" makes it easier for the right person to recognize that you can help.

You may also need examples of your work, but they do not have to come from paid clients. A writer can create sample articles, a designer can make example graphics, and a virtual assistant can show sample spreadsheets using fictional information.

Once someone is interested, agree on what you will provide, the price, the deadline, how revisions will be handled, and when payment is due. Clear expectations keep a small project from turning into far more work than you agreed to do.

Freelance platforms and teaching sites are best viewed as something you build over time. For faster income, start with people you know and local businesses that may already need your skills. For income that can keep growing, begin building your presence on larger platforms at the same time.

6.3 PART-TIME AND SEASONAL JOBS

Most people already know that getting a part-time job is one way to earn extra money. That does not mean it should be dismissed as too obvious. There are more part-time options available than many people realize, and if you have some time to work and genuinely need additional income, it is worth exploring them.

Retail stores, restaurants, hotels, warehouses, grocery stores, schools, gyms, entertainment venues, and local businesses all hire part-time workers. Seasonal openings increase around holidays, summer travel, festivals, sporting events, and other busy periods. Some employers need people only on weekends, evenings, early mornings, or during a specific season.

A part-time job does not have to be a lifetime commitment. It can simply be something you do for a few months to catch up on bills, pay off a specific expense, rebuild your savings, or get through a financially difficult period. You are allowed to use a job for what you need from it and move on when it no longer fits.

One of the biggest advantages is predictability. You generally know your hourly rate, when you are scheduled, and when you will be paid. That can be especially valuable if the uncertainty of gig work would make an already stressful financial situation worse. Some part-time jobs also come with employee discounts, free meals, tuition assistance, paid time off, or other benefits that reduce expenses.

The downside is that getting hired takes time. You may need to complete an application, attend an interview, provide references, pass a background check, and wait for a start date. You may apply and never hear back, or an employer may choose someone else. Apply to several places rather than waiting on one response before moving to the next.

If speed matters, look for employers advertising immediate openings, open interviews, seasonal hiring events, or several available positions. Be clear about your availability, particularly if you can work hours that are harder to fill, such as weekends, early mornings, evenings, or holidays.

Do not limit yourself to retail or food service. A library may need weekend help, a gym may need someone at the front desk, or a school may need cafeteria or after-school workers. Search local job boards broadly and notice businesses in your area that may be hiring.

The main tradeoff is control. With a part-time job, an employer decides when you are scheduled and what work you will do. In exchange, you may receive steadier hours, clearer pay expectations, and fewer work-related expenses than many gig or freelance options require. If you need reliable extra income and can commit to a schedule, a part-time job may be the better choice.

6.4 TEMP AGENCIES AND INDEPENDENT CONTRACT LISTINGS

Not everyone wants or is able to commit to a regular part-time job. If you are looking for temporary work, temp agencies and independent contract listings can be a good middle ground.

They often provide steadier work than one-time gigs without requiring a long-term commitment to a single employer.

Temp agencies, also known as staffing agencies, connect workers with employers that need help for a limited period of time. A good agency may place you within days when an employer needs help quickly. Assignments can last one day, a few weeks, several months, or sometimes turn into a permanent position. You may need to complete an application, interview, skills assessment, background check, or drug screening before you are eligible for work.

Once you are registered, respond quickly when the agency contacts you. Workers who are dependable, show up on time, and do a good job are often offered more assignments because the agency knows it can rely on them. It can also be worth registering with more than one staffing agency, since each one works with different employers and may have access to different opportunities.

Temp agencies are not the only place to find temporary opportunities. There is also a wider world of contract work that does not fit neatly into a gig app or a traditional part-time job. I once found an independent contractor position on Craigslist with a real estate technology startup. I did not have a real estate license or any previous experience in real estate, but I responded to the posting anyway. The company was looking for someone who could use a smartphone, follow directions, and show up reliably. I could set my own schedule, and my job was to show available apartments to prospective renters. It paid $10 per showing, and often multiple showings were scheduled close together, so the money added up nicely. It was flexible paid work that fit my life at the time, and it was not the kind of opportunity I even knew existed until I came across the listing.

Unfortunately, the company went out of business during the pandemic, so the job did not last. But the experience taught me something important: there are all kinds of unusual opportunities out there that you may never think to search for by name. Sometimes you discover them simply by browsing contract listings with an open mind and considering work that falls outside the jobs you would normally search for.

Searching broadly can uncover event setup and teardown, mystery shopping, local inspection work, merchandising, inventory projects, convention staffing, product demonstrations, apartment showings, and other jobs that may exist only in certain places or seasons. Try terms such as "temporary," "contract," "independent contractor," "seasonal," "weekend," or "flexible schedule," along with the type of work you are willing to do.

These opportunities can be less predictable than a traditional part-time job, and some assignments may end with little notice. Still, they can be an excellent option when you need work quickly, want income for a limited period, or enjoy variety instead of committing to the same role every week. The more broadly you search, the more likely you are to discover opportunities you never knew existed.

6.5 WHAT TO KNOW BEFORE YOU START

The choices in this chapter come with different tradeoffs. Understanding those tradeoffs can help you choose the option that actually fits your life, your schedule, and your financial situation.

Gig work usually offers the most flexibility. You can often choose your own hours, work more when you need extra money, and stop when your schedule changes. Some apps also let you access your earnings quickly. The downside is that income can vary, work is not guaranteed, and vehicle-based gigs come with real operating costs.

A part-time job offers less flexibility but more predictability. You usually know when you are scheduled, what your hourly rate is, and when your paycheck will arrive. Taxes are typically withheld automatically, and some employers offer benefits, discounts, or other perks. The downside is that getting hired can take time, and you have less control over your schedule.

Freelance and contract work can offer higher pay for specialized skills and may eventually lead to repeat clients. Over time, it can provide both flexibility and more consistent income. But it usually takes more effort to find customers, build reviews, and create steady demand. Platform fees, delayed payouts, and unpaid time spent looking for work can also reduce what you actually earn.

Before choosing, look beyond the advertised pay and ask what the work will really cost you. Driving has gas, maintenance, tolls, insurance, and wear on your vehicle. Freelancing may require software, supplies, advertising, or platform fees. A part-time job may involve commuting, uniforms, meals away from home, or childcare. The best option is not always the one with the highest number attached to it. Sometimes it is the one that leaves you with the most useful income after the real costs are considered, or the one that fits into your life most easily.

Taxes are another important difference. Traditional employees usually have taxes withheld from each paycheck. Gig workers, freelancers, and many independent contractors generally do not. If taxes are not being withheld, you will probably need to set aside part of each payment instead of treating the full amount as spendable. The exact amount depends on your income, location, and personal tax situation, so check the rules that apply to you or ask a tax professional for guidance.

Simple records can make all of this easier. Track what you earn, platform fees, mileage, supplies, software, advertising, and other work-related expenses from the beginning. A spreadsheet, mileage app, notebook, or separate bank account can help you see what you are truly earning and make tax time less stressful.

The best choice may change over time. Gig work might help you immediately while you wait to begin a part-time job. A temporary assignment might cover the next two months while you build freelance clients. A seasonal job might help you pay off a bill without requiring a longer commitment. These options do not have to compete with one another. They can work together.

The important thing is to put something in motion. Apply, create the profile, register with the agency, or send the message. The opportunities in this chapter may not pay as quickly as selling something from your home, but they can create something the earlier chapters could not: a source of extra money that continues after this week is over.

CHAPTER 7
THE MONEY YOU'RE ALREADY SPENDING

Every chapter so far has focused on bringing more money in. This chapter looks at the other half of the equation: the money already leaving your hands. That part gets talked about far less, but it can make just as much difference, especially when money is quietly disappearing every week on things you may barely notice anymore.

I know this from experience. At different points in my life, I have had to learn how to live on much less than I was used to. It was not a deliberate minimalist experiment. It was simply what the situation required. There was an amount of money coming in, a set of bills that had to be paid, and a lifestyle that could no longer continue without something changing.

So things changed. Subscriptions I had kept for years were canceled in a single afternoon. Meals that used to come from a delivery app started coming from my own kitchen. I started grocery shopping at Aldi instead of Whole Foods and drinking instant coffee instead of stopping at Starbucks.

What surprised me most was not how hard those changes were. It was how little I missed most of them once they were gone. A lot of what I cut had become automatic instead of meaningful. It was spending I had stopped noticing because it had become part of my routine, not because it was making my life noticeably better. Cutting it did not feel like deprivation as often as I expected. Most of the time, it felt like finally paying attention to something I had allowed to run on autopilot for years.

The funny thing is that many of those changes never changed back. I still shop at Aldi and cook most meals at home. I still drink instant coffee instead of stopping at Starbucks every morning. Not because I have to anymore, but because I realized I was not giving up as much as I thought. I was spending less, and my day-to-day life still felt fine.

7.1 EVERY DOLLAR HAS THE SAME JOB

One of the biggest mental shifts I ever made was realizing that earning an extra dollar and keeping an extra dollar accomplish exactly the same thing. Your bank account doesn't care where the dollar came from. It only knows whether it's there.

That sounds obvious, but most of us naturally focus on the earning side of the equation. We spend hours looking for ways to make more money while barely giving a second thought to the money quietly flowing out of our accounts every month. Meanwhile, recurring charges, impulse purchases, and everyday habits continue taking money out of our accounts almost unnoticed.

The difference is that earning more usually requires more time and more effort. You have to work another shift, complete another gig, sell another item, or find another client. Cutting an unnecessary expense often takes just a few minutes. Cancel a subscription you don't use, switch your phone plan, shop somewhere less expensive, or stop buying something that has quietly become a habit instead of a conscious choice, and the savings continue month after month without any additional effort.

The first step is simply knowing where your money is actually going. You can't fix spending you don't notice. Most people could probably tell you roughly what they spend on rent or a car payment, but far fewer could tell you how much they spent last month on coffee, takeout, streaming services, convenience store snacks, or online impulse purchases. Individually, those expenses don't seem like much. Together, they can easily add up to hundreds of dollars every month.

The good news is that there are dozens of places to save money, and not all of them require making big sacrifices. You might save by shopping at a different grocery store, negotiating your internet bill, changing insurance companies, canceling memberships you forgot you had, planning meals before grocery shopping, buying generic brands, or simply waiting twenty-four hours before making a purchase. None of these changes will make you rich overnight, but together they can make a noticeable difference.

That doesn't mean every expense should be cut. Some things are absolutely worth spending money on because they are genuinely needed or actually improve your quality of life. The goal isn't to spend as little as possible. The goal is to spend intentionally. If something brings you real value, keep it. If it has become an automatic expense that no longer adds much to your life, it may be worth reconsidering.

As you'll see throughout this chapter, finding an extra $100 isn't always about earning another $100. Sometimes it's about realizing you were already spending it. Once you know where your money is going, you can decide where you'd rather have it go instead.

With that in mind, challenge yourself to find $100 you can cut from your budget this week. It doesn't have to come from one big change. It might be ten small changes that save $10 each, or two changes that save $50 each. However you get there, treat it like a game. See if you can finish this chapter with an extra $100 that was already yours all along.

7.2 THE SUBSCRIPTIONS AND MEMBERSHIPS YOU FORGOT YOU HAD

The easiest place to begin is with your recurring expenses. The savings here usually don't require you to change your daily habits. You don't have to stop drinking coffee or eating out. They simply require twenty or thirty minutes and a willingness to take an honest look at where your money is already going.

The problem with subscriptions is that they quietly disappear into the background. The decision to sign up happened months or even years ago, but the money keeps leaving your account long after you've stopped thinking about it. Automatic payments are convenient when you're actively using something. They're expensive when you've forgotten they're there.

Streaming services are probably the most obvious example. Maybe you signed up for Netflix years ago, then added Disney+ because the kids wanted it. Later you subscribed to another service to watch one particular show, and before long you're paying for four or five different streaming platforms every month. Do you really need cable, Netflix, Disney+, Hulu, Max, Paramount+, and Amazon Prime Video all at the same time?

For most people, the answer is probably no.

That doesn't mean you can never watch those shows again. It simply means you don't have to pay for every service every month. One option is to rotate them. Watch everything you want on one service, cancel it, then subscribe to another for a month or two. By the time you come back, there will be new shows waiting for you, and you'll have saved a surprising amount of money over the course of the year.

App subscriptions deserve the same scrutiny. Many of us pay a few dollars every month for apps we downloaded because they seemed useful at the time. Maybe it's a photo editing app, a meditation app, a workout program, extra cloud storage, or a premium version of a budgeting app. Ask yourself honestly: when was the last time you actually opened it? If you don't remember, you're probably paying for something you no longer use.

The same goes for subscription boxes. They always seem exciting when you first sign up. A monthly box of snacks, fruit, wine, beauty products, coffee, or pet toys sounds like a fun surprise. But after a while the excitement wears off while the monthly charge quietly keeps showing up. If you wouldn't sign up for it today, why are you still paying for it?

Gym memberships are another common example. If you're going three or four times a week, keep it. You're getting your money's worth. But if you've been meaning to go "next Monday" for the past six months, it may be time to admit you're paying for the idea of exercising rather than actually exercising.

Not every recurring expense can simply be canceled. You still need car insurance, cell phone service, internet service, electricity, water, and other basic utilities. But that doesn't mean you have to accept whatever you're currently paying. It may be worth comparing insurance quotes, looking at lower-cost cell phone plans, asking your internet provider about promotional rates, shopping around when contracts end, or looking for discounts you qualify for. Even if you keep the same services, paying a little less each month can add up to hundreds of dollars over the course of a year.

I learned this lesson with my own car insurance. At one point, I was paying hundreds of dollars every month because I had simply renewed the same policy year after year without looking at it closely. When I needed to cut expenses, I finally compared quotes from other companies and reviewed what my policy actually covered. By switching insurers and adjusting my plan, I saved a significant amount of money without leaving myself underinsured.

Car insurance is one of those expenses that many people set up once and rarely think about again. But your needs can change over time. If you drive very little, work from home, have an older vehicle, or have built up an emergency fund, it may be worth reviewing your policy to see whether you're paying for coverage you no longer need or whether a higher deductible makes sense for your situation. Every person's needs are different, so don't reduce coverage just to save money. Instead, take a fresh look at what you're paying for and make sure it still matches your life today. Many people discover they're spending far more on car insurance than necessary simply because they never stopped to ask whether their policy still made sense.

There are plenty of other recurring expenses worth reviewing as well. Music streaming services. Audiobook memberships. Gaming subscriptions. Online newspapers and magazines. Professional memberships. Warehouse clubs. Meal planning apps. Even Amazon Prime deserves an honest look. If you're paying for it but only order a few things each year, is it really worth the annual fee?

None of these expenses are bad on their own. If you genuinely use them and they improve your life, keep them. The goal isn't to eliminate everything you enjoy or make yourself miserable just to save a few dollars. The goal is to make sure you're spending your money intentionally.

A simple way to decide is to ask yourself two questions for every recurring expense:

Can I find a less expensive way to get the same thing?

Or can I comfortably live without it?

Maybe you don't need cable and three streaming services. Maybe one or two is enough. Perhaps you don't need the premium version of an app you haven't opened in months. Maybe that warehouse club membership made sense when you had a larger family, but today you're paying an annual fee you barely use.

The exercise here is simple. Pull up one or two months of bank or credit card statements and write down every recurring charge you can find. Don't rely on memory. Memory has a funny way of remembering the expenses that feel important while conveniently forgetting the ones you barely notice. Your bank statement doesn't have that problem.

Once you have the list in front of you, look at each expense honestly.

Are you still using it?

Is it still worth what you pay for it?

Could you live without it, even temporarily?

Is there a less expensive way to get the same thing?

Those questions help you evaluate each recurring expense based on the value it adds to your life today, not the reason you signed up months or years ago. Some expenses will still make sense. Others may be ready to cancel, pause, downgrade, or replace with a less expensive alternative.

The point is not to eliminate everything. In fact, I wouldn't recommend it. But chances are you'll find at least a few subscriptions, memberships, or recurring expenses that have quietly outlived their usefulness. Those are some of the easiest dollars you'll ever save because nothing about your daily life really changes. The only thing that changes is that your bank account stops paying for decisions you made months or years ago that no longer fit your life today.

7.3 THE SMALL SPENDING THAT ADDS UP QUIETLY

This category is a little more sensitive than subscriptions because it touches habits, routines, and everyday comforts. It is worth approaching without shame. If you are struggling financially, honesty matters more than embarrassment. The goal is not to criticize yourself for what you bought, but to understand where your money is going so you can make choices that actually help.

A coffee on the way to work. Lunch picked up instead of packed. A food delivery order on a night when you are too tired to cook. A quick stop at the convenience store. A small online purchase because it was only $12. None of these purchases feel significant in the moment, and on their own, they usually are not. The issue is the quiet accumulation of dozens of small decisions across a month, each one reasonable by itself, adding up to a number that is often much larger than people realize.

The goal of this section is not to judge every purchase. It is simply to notice them. For one or two weeks, track the money you spend outside your regular bills. You can use a notebook, a notes app, a spreadsheet, or your banking app. The method does not matter as much as the honesty. Write down the coffee, the delivery fee, the snack, the app purchase, the extra item tossed into your cart, and the quick stop you barely thought about. You may be surprised by what you discover.

Delivery apps deserve a specific mention because they make the true cost of eating out easy to miss. What looks like a fifteen-dollar meal can quickly become twenty-five or thirty dollars once the delivery fee, service fee, taxes, and tip are added. Do that two or three times a week, and you may spend several hundred dollars a month without ever making a single large purchase.

Online shopping deserves an honest look too. There is nothing wrong with buying things online when you genuinely need them. But if money is tight, pay attention to how often you make purchases simply because something is on sale, looks useful, or is only a few dollars. Those small purchases can be surprisingly easy to justify in the moment, especially when they take only a few clicks. Individually they may not seem like much, but over the course of a month they can quietly add up to far more than you expected.

Once you start paying attention, you can decide deliberately which habits are worth keeping and which ones you would rather change. Maybe the coffee stays and the delivery orders go. Maybe it is the other way around. The point is not to eliminate every small comfort. It is to make sure the ones you keep are the ones you have actually chosen, rather than the ones that have quietly become automatic.

Not every expense happens every week, though. Some spending shows up only once in a while, which makes it easy to overlook until the money is already spent. Haircuts, pet grooming, vet visits, oil changes, car repairs, prescriptions, eyeglasses, dental cleanings, school supplies, birthday gifts, clothing, shoes, dry cleaning, lawn care, home maintenance, and appliance repairs can all add up over time.

These are not unnecessary expenses. You still need a haircut. Your dog still deserves good care. Your car and home still need to be maintained. The question is not whether you should stop paying for these things. The question is whether you are paying more than you need to.

Maybe you have been going to the same salon for years without ever comparing prices. Maybe another barber across town charges less for a haircut that is just as good. Maybe your dog gets groomed every month at the first place you ever tried, even though another groomer offers the same service for less. Maybe a repair, prescription, or pair of glasses could be found at a lower price if you compared a few options before paying.

For purchases that are not urgent, it helps to give yourself a little space before spending the money. Waiting twenty-four hours before buying something gives you time to separate what you actually need from what only felt important in the moment. Sometimes you will still decide to buy it. Other times, you may realize you can wait, borrow it, buy it used, find a less expensive version, or skip it completely.

Small spending is not the enemy. Unnoticed spending is. Once you begin paying attention to where your money is going, you can stop guessing and start making decisions that fit your priorities instead of your habits.

7.4 WHEN THE BIG EXPENSES ARE THE REAL PROBLEM

So far, this chapter has focused on the expenses that are easiest to review first: subscriptions, memberships, utilities, small daily purchases, and the spending that adds up quietly. Those changes matter. They can free up real money, and they are often the best place to begin.

But for some people, the smaller expenses are not the main problem.

If you have gone through the exercises honestly and the math still does not work, it may be time to look at the largest expenses in your life. Housing, a car payment, insurance, debt payments, or anything else that takes up a large share of your income every month can overwhelm the rest of your budget.

This is a harder conversation than canceling a subscription or cutting back on delivery orders. A home that costs more than your income can comfortably support, or a car payment that takes too much of your paycheck before anything else is paid, usually cannot be fixed with a cheaper streaming plan. Smaller cuts may help, but they may not be enough if one major expense is creating most of the pressure.

If this describes your situation, it may be worth asking bigger questions.

Is there a less expensive place to live?

Would a roommate make sense for a period of time?

Could you move closer to work or family support?

Is your car payment too high for your current income?

Would selling or refinancing the car be worth exploring?

Is there a debt payment or loan that needs a more serious plan?

None of these decisions should be made quickly or out of panic. Moving, changing cars, taking on a roommate, or adjusting major financial obligations can affect your comfort, safety, family, work, and long-term finances. This is not the same as canceling an unused app. It deserves time, research, and, when possible, guidance from someone you trust.

But it would be dishonest not to mention it. For some readers, no amount of selling old items, skipping coffee, or picking up gig work will fully solve a budget that is being crushed by one large expense. If that is your situation, the most helpful thing you can do is name the problem clearly instead of treating it like a personal failure.

You may want to talk with a trusted friend, a financial counselor, your lender, your landlord, or another qualified professional about what your real options are. You do not have to know the answer immediately. The first step is simply being willing to look directly at the biggest numbers in your life and ask whether they still fit the income and circumstances you have today.

7.5 BUILDING A SIMPLE BUDGET YOU'LL ACTUALLY FOLLOW

For some people, the word *budget* immediately brings to mind spreadsheets, complicated formulas, and recording every dollar they spend. If that works for you, great. But for many people, that kind of budgeting feels so overwhelming that they avoid it altogether.

A budget does not have to be complicated to be useful.

At its core, a budget is simply a plan for where your money will go before you spend it. It gives every dollar a purpose instead of leaving you to wonder where it all disappeared at the end of the month.

The truth is that you already have a budget, whether you've written one down or not. If your paycheck comes in, your bills get paid, you buy groceries, and whatever is left gets spent however it happens to get spent, that's still a budget. It's just one that's happening by default instead of by design.

The goal is to change that.

Start with your monthly income after taxes. Then write down your essential expenses first. Housing. Utilities. Transportation. Insurance. Groceries. Debt payments. Anything that must be paid before you can think about the rest.

Next, add the expenses that matter to you personally. Maybe that's a gym membership you actually use, a streaming service you enjoy, a monthly dinner out with friends, or money you want to set aside for a hobby. Remember, the goal isn't to eliminate everything you enjoy. It's to make sure your spending reflects what is actually important to you.

Finally, decide where you want the money that's left to go. Maybe it's building an emergency fund. Maybe it's paying down debt. Maybe it's saving for a vacation, replacing your car, or simply creating a little breathing room so the next unexpected expense doesn't become a crisis.

Keep the system as simple as possible. You don't need twenty spending categories if five will do. Some people prefer a spreadsheet. Others use a budgeting app. Some people keep a notebook or use separate checking and savings accounts. The best budget is the one you'll actually use consistently.

Don't expect to get it perfect the first month. Almost nobody does. You'll forget expenses, underestimate others, and probably spend more in some categories than you planned. That's normal. A budget isn't a test you either pass or fail. It's a tool that gets better every time you adjust it.

One thing that helped me was treating my savings like any other bill. Instead of waiting to see if there was money left over at the end of the month, I decided how much I wanted to save first and moved that money as soon as I got paid. Even if it was only a small amount, it helped me build the habit of paying myself before spending on things that were less important.

Review your budget once a month. Life changes. Prices change. Income changes. Your budget should change too. Something that made sense six months ago may not make sense today, and that's okay. The goal isn't to create a perfect budget you'll follow forever. The goal is to build a flexible plan that helps you spend with intention instead of reacting to whatever comes along.

A budget should make your life feel less stressful, not more. If it's so detailed that you dread looking at it, simplify it. If it's so loose that it doesn't help you make decisions, tighten it up a little. The right budget is the one that gives you confidence, helps you reach your goals, and is simple enough that you'll still be using it a year from now.

CHAPTER 8
MATCHING THE METHOD TO YOUR LIFE

By now, you've seen a real range of ways to make extra money: things to sell, tasks to do, gig work, more structured part-time options, and a closer look at the money already going out the door. That is a lot of ground covered, and it is worth pausing before going any further to talk about something just as important as any single method: how to pick the right one for your specific life.

This chapter is not going to introduce a new method. It is going to help you choose among the ones you've already seen, because choosing well is its own skill, separate from knowing the options exist in the first place.

8.1 THERE'S NO UNIVERSAL "BEST" OPTION

It's worth saying plainly what has been implied throughout this book: there is no single best way to make $100 this week. Every method in the chapters before this one has worked for someone, often very well. Every one of them has also been the wrong fit for someone else.

That matters because it is easy to fall into a trap without realizing it. When you read a list of options, some of them may sound more impressive than others. Freelancing may sound more sophisticated than selling an old coffee maker. Driving for a rideshare app may sound more like "real work" than babysitting a neighbor's kids for an evening. But how impressive something sounds has very little to do with whether it is actually right for your life.

The right method is not the one that sounds best when you describe it to someone else. It is the one you can actually start this week, given your real schedule, your real preferences, your real responsibilities, and your real circumstances. If you only have two free evenings, your best option may look very different from someone who has full days available. If you hate driving, delivery apps may not be the right fit. If you need money quickly, building a freelance profile may be useful later, but selling something you already own may help sooner.

This is why choosing matters. A method that fits your life is easier to start, easier to stick with, and much less likely to drain the energy you need for everything else. A method that looks good on paper but fights your schedule, personality, or resources can make you feel like you failed, even when the real problem was simply that you picked the wrong tool for the job.

This connects back to Chapter 3, where we talked about the method mattering far less than the decision itself. This chapter does not contradict that idea. It builds on it. The decision is still the load-bearing part. But once you have decided to act, you still need to choose a specific path. The decision gets you to the starting line. This chapter is about figuring out which direction to run.

8.2 WHAT YOUR SCHEDULE ACTUALLY ALLOWS

The first real filter is the most practical one: what does your actual week look like, and which options fit inside it?

This is not just about ruling things out. It is also about noticing what might realistically work. Your schedule may close the door on some methods, but it can also point you toward the ones that fit most naturally.

If you work a rigid nine-to-five with little flexibility, daytime options like showing apartments during business hours or attending a lengthy in-person research study may be hard to make work, no matter how appealing they sound. But evening and weekend options may fit much better. Delivery driving after work, selling items you can photograph and list during a lunch break, or picking up weekend work might match that kind of schedule more naturally.

If you work unpredictable shifts, the opposite may be true. A regular part-time job with fixed hours could be difficult if your schedule already changes week to week. In that case, something flexible, like gig app work, selling items online, or short contract assignments, may work better because it lets you act when you actually have time available.

If you are caring for kids, an aging parent, or anyone else who needs your attention during the day, that changes the math again. Plasma donation or an in-person research study that requires sitting somewhere for an hour or more may be hard to arrange without backup care. But selling items locally, listing things online, answering messages from your phone, or doing small tasks in short bursts may fit more naturally into the cracks of an already full day.

If you do not have reliable access to a car, driving and most delivery work may not be realistic, no matter how good the pay looks for someone who does have a vehicle. That is not a failure on your part. It is simply a real constraint. Once you recognize it, you can stop wasting energy on options that do not fit and look instead at what might work: selling items, offering a service from home, tutoring online, applying for nearby part-time work, or finding opportunities you can reach by walking, biking, public transportation, or rides from someone you trust.

It helps to write out your week, hour by hour if needed, rather than estimating from memory how much free time you have. Most people are surprised in one direction or the other once they see it on paper. Some discover they have less open time than they assumed once commuting, sleep, caregiving, and existing obligations are accounted for honestly. Others discover small pockets they had stopped noticing, like a lunch break that is actually free, an evening that could be used once a week, or a weekend morning that has been claimed by habit rather than by anything that truly has to happen then.

Either way, seeing the real shape of your week makes your choice clearer. You are not trying to find the option that sounds best in theory. You are trying to find the one that fits the life you are actually living right now.

None of this is about which methods are good or bad in some abstract sense. It is about matching the method to your real schedule, real responsibilities, and real constraints. When you do that, you are much more likely to choose something you can actually start, follow through on, and keep using long enough for it to help.

8.3 WHAT YOU'RE ACTUALLY WILLING TO DO

The next filter is more personal: what are you actually willing to do?

This is where honesty matters again. Every method in this book asks something different of you. Some require talking to strangers. Some require selling your belongings. Some involve driving, teaching, physical work, or spending time on a computer. None of those things are right or wrong. The question is whether they are a good fit for you.

Maybe you genuinely do not want to sell your belongings to strangers. Maybe driving at night makes you uncomfortable. Maybe the idea of constantly messaging customers on a task app sounds exhausting. Maybe donating plasma is simply not something you are willing to do. Those are all perfectly reasonable preferences.

The important thing is to separate a real preference from an excuse. We talked about this back in Chapter 1. Saying, "I don't have any skills," or "Nothing will work for me," usually falls apart once you examine it honestly. But saying, "I don't want to drive strangers around," or "I don't want to spend my evenings away from my family," is different. Those preferences often remain true even after you've thought them through, and they deserve to be respected.

Pay attention to how you feel when you imagine doing the work. If a method makes you uncomfortable because it is simply new, that feeling will often fade once you get started. But if the method clashes with your values, personality, or lifestyle, forcing yourself through it every week is unlikely to be sustainable.

Remember, this book is full of options. You do not have to make every method work. You only need to find one that fits your life well enough that you will actually follow through. The best method is not the one someone else loves. It is the one you are genuinely willing to do.

8.4 STACK ONCE YOU'VE STARTED, NOT BEFORE

Once you have one method working, adding a second or even a third can help you reach your goal faster. The important part of that sentence is *once you have one method working.*

This is not permission to abandon the One-Thing Principle from Chapter 2. That principle still applies at the beginning. If you have not chosen a path and actually started it yet, trying to list ten items for sale, sign up for three gig apps, build a freelance profile, and apply for part-time jobs all in the same week is not stacking. It is the same multitasking trap we talked about earlier, and it usually leads to a lot of activity but very little progress.

That said, starting one path does not always mean taking only one small action. If your chosen option involves waiting for someone else to respond, such as applying for a part-time job, registering with a temp agency, applying for a research study, or pitching freelance clients, it often makes sense to submit several applications or proposals. That is still one focused direction. You are not spreading yourself across unrelated opportunities. You are giving your chosen path multiple chances to succeed.

Stacking happens after you have some experience with the first option. Once you have listed a few items for sale, completed your first gig shift, finished a research study, or landed a freelance client, you understand what that work actually requires. You know how much time it takes, how much energy it uses, and whether it fits your life. At that point, adding another small source of income is less likely to scatter your attention. Instead, it builds on what you have already learned.

For example, you might continue selling items while driving for a delivery app on weekends. You might work a temporary job while gradually building a freelance business. You might pick up a part-time job and continue selling a few things online whenever you have time. Each income source supports the others instead of competing with them.

Think of it like building a fire. Trying to light five small fires with one match usually leaves you with five fires that never really catch. It is much easier to get one fire burning first and then use it to light the next one. The same idea applies here. Build momentum first, then expand.

If you are just getting started this week, keep your focus on one approach. Choose the one that best fits your schedule, your preferences, and your circumstances, and follow it through. If that approach requires waiting, take several focused actions within that same category to improve your chances of success. Once you have some experience and your first income source is producing results, you can begin stacking additional opportunities without overwhelming yourself.

8.5 A SIMPLE WAY TO DECIDE THIS WEEK

After everything you've read so far, you might still be wondering, *"So...which one should I actually do?"*

Instead of looking for the perfect answer, start by looking at what is actually possible. The best opportunity is usually the one that fits your life right now, not the one that sounds the most exciting or pays the most in theory.

Start by asking yourself a few simple questions.

How much time do I realistically have this week? Not the week you wish you had, but the one that's actually on your calendar. Do you have a free weekend? A few evenings? An hour during lunch? Your available time immediately narrows the list.

What resources do I already have? Do you have a reliable car? A computer? A smartphone? Things you no longer need that you could sell? A particular skill or experience that someone would pay for? Focus on what you can use right now, not what you might learn or build someday. New skills can create opportunities down the road, but this week's plan should start with the resources you already have.

What am I genuinely willing to do? If you hate driving, don't choose a rideshare app just because someone else makes good money doing it. If you enjoy working with people, tutoring or customer service may be a better fit. If you'd rather work alone, selling items or freelancing might feel more natural. You are far more likely to follow through with something that fits your personality than something you dread from the beginning.

How quickly do I need the money? If you need cash in the next day or two, selling things you already own or completing a local task may be the best option. If you have a little more time, applying for part-time work, registering with a temp agency, or building a freelance profile may create more consistent income over the weeks ahead.

Once you've answered those questions, look back at the options covered in the previous chapters. You can also use the list of 300 money-making ideas at the end of this book, or come up with an idea of your own.

Then stop looking for more options and choose one.

If you have several things you can sell, list at least one of them today. If gig work fits your schedule, complete the application and schedule your first shift. If you want a part-time job, submit applications to several employers instead of waiting to hear back from just one. If freelancing is your goal, create your profile and send your first proposals. If you genuinely do not want to add anything else to your schedule right now, go back to Chapter 7 and look for ways to spend less. Cutting an expense may not feel as exciting as earning new money, but it can solve the same problem.

The point is not to find the single best way to make an extra $100. The point is to be honest about your circumstances and choose something you can actually start today. Look at your real schedule, your real responsibilities, your real resources, and your real financial situation. Then pick the option that fits well enough to begin. Getting started with something imperfect will help you more than waiting for the perfect plan.

If you can answer one simple question, you're ready to begin:

"Given the life I have today, what is the best step I can take this week?"

Then take it.

A week from now, you can always adjust your plan. You can try something different, add another income source, or build on what's already working. But none of that happens until you start.

The goal has never been to make the perfect decision. It has always been to make a decision and follow through.

CHAPTER 9

WHEN TO SCALE, WHEN TO QUIT, WHEN TO PIVOT

By now, if you have followed through on anything from the earlier chapters, you have something most people never get: real experience. Maybe it went well. Maybe it did not go the way you hoped. Maybe it landed somewhere in between, close but not quite right.

Whatever happened, you are no longer guessing. You have actual information about what works for you, what drains you, what fits your schedule, and what produces results. That puts you in a much stronger position than someone who is still only thinking about getting started.

This chapter is about what to do with that information. Once you have tried something, three honest paths open up. You can scale it, quit it, or pivot to something that fits better. The challenge is knowing which path you are actually standing on.

There is a reason this chapter comes near the end of the book. Everything before this point was about getting you to take action: shifting your mindset, exploring the options, choosing something realistic, and matching the method to your life. But once you have acted, the question changes.

Now it is not, *What should I try?*

It is, *What did I learn, and what should I do next?*

This chapter will help you answer that.

9.1 THE THREE SIGNALS WORTH PAYING ATTENTION TO

After you make a real attempt at any method in this book, you will usually land in one of three places. Learning to recognize which one you are in matters because each one calls for a different next move.

The first signal is simple: **it is working.** You tried something, it brought in money, and it did not completely drain you in the process. Maybe you sold a few items faster than expected. Maybe your first delivery shift went well. Maybe a freelance client responded, a part-time job called you back, or cutting expenses freed up more money than you thought it would. When something works, the next question is not whether to abandon it. The next question is whether there is more opportunity there.

The second signal is the opposite: **it is not working.** You gave it a real chance, but it is not paying off. Maybe no one is responding to your listings. Maybe the gig app in your area is too slow. Maybe the platform is overcrowded, the schedule does not fit, or the money is too inconsistent to be worth the time. This does not automatically mean you failed. Sometimes the method is simply not a good match for your location, your schedule, your resources, or the demand around you.

The third signal is more subtle: **it is close.** Something about the approach is almost right, but not quite. Maybe selling items works, but the platform you chose is not getting much traffic. Maybe delivery driving pays well, but only during certain hours. Maybe freelancing seems promising, but your profile or pricing needs work. Maybe cutting expenses helped, but you need to look at a different category of spending. When something is close, you may not need to quit. You may need to adjust.

This is where many people get tripped up. They do not pause long enough to read the signal. They quit too early because they feel frustrated, or they keep pushing because they do not want to admit something is not working. Both reactions are understandable, but neither one is always useful.

A better approach is to ask, "What is this attempt actually telling me?"

If it is working, consider scaling it. If it is not working after a fair try, consider letting it go. If it is close, look for the adjustment that might make it fit better.

The rest of this chapter is about learning how to tell the difference before you react.

9.2 WHEN IT'S WORKING: DECIDING WHETHER TO SCALE

If your first attempt worked, congratulations. You solved the hardest part: getting started.

Now you have another decision to make. Should you simply keep going, or should you try to make it something bigger?

Before answering that, make sure you have enough information. One successful sale, one good delivery shift, or one freelance client is encouraging, but it is not necessarily a trend. Give it another week or two if you can. A single good result tells you something is possible. Several consistent results tell you whether it is reliable.

If it keeps working, your first choice may simply be to keep doing it.

That may sound obvious, but it is often overlooked. If selling items is working, keep listing items. If driving for a delivery app fits your schedule and earns the income you expected, keep driving. If tutoring, freelancing, or a part-time job is helping you reach your goal, there is nothing wrong with simply continuing to do it. You do not need a new strategy every week. Sometimes the smartest move is to keep doing what is already working.

In many cases, continuing is easier than starting something new. You have already learned the process. You know how much time it takes, what to expect, and how it fits into your life. Instead of climbing another learning curve, you can build on the experience you already have.

Scaling means trying to earn more from something that has already proven itself. Sometimes that means putting in more time, such as driving an extra evening each week, accepting another shift, taking on another freelance client, tutoring one more student, or completing more projects.

Other times, scaling means improving the way you do the work. You might learn which hours pay best, raise your rates after gaining experience, offer an additional service to existing clients, move from one platform to two, ask satisfied customers for referrals, improve your profile, respond faster to leads, or create a simple system that helps you complete the work more efficiently.

Scaling may also require learning more. This is actually the time when more research and practice can help, because you are no longer researching from zero. You have experience to build on. You may need to understand pricing, improve your communication, compare platforms, learn what customers expect, or figure out how to earn more without adding as many extra hours.

Scaling often asks for more than repeating the same first step, but now you have a better idea of what is worth learning next.

Many people who are successful did not start with a perfect plan. They started with one small thing, learned from it, and improved as they went. The first version may have been messy, underpriced, inefficient, or uncertain. But because they kept paying attention, they learned what worked, adjusted what did not, and slowly became better at earning from the same opportunity.

The important thing is not to rush that decision. Scaling requires more than one week of experience. Give yourself time to learn the work, understand what it pays, and decide whether you actually enjoy it before committing more time and energy.

Remember what we talked about in Chapter 3. This book was written to help you solve a financial problem, not to convince you to build a business. If earning an extra $100 solved the problem you needed to solve, you are allowed to stop. If you enjoy the work and want to keep going, that is a great option too.

There is one final trap worth mentioning. Once people discover something that works, they sometimes feel like they *should* keep growing it simply because they can. But the ability to scale and the desire to scale are two different things. Some people are perfectly happy earning a little extra money when they need it. Others enjoy turning a small opportunity into something much bigger.

Neither choice is better.

The goal is not to build the biggest income stream possible. The goal is to build one that fits your life.

9.3 WHEN IT'S NOT WORKING: DECIDING TO QUIT

Sometimes, after you give something a real try, the answer is clear: this is not the right fit.

That does not always mean it failed to make money. Something can bring in income and still cost too much in other ways. You might earn an extra $500 a week delivering food, but the late nights could be putting a strain on your marriage. You might find freelance clients, but feel constantly stressed by the pressure to keep finding the next project. You might make money driving, but realize the wear and tear on your car is more than you expected.

Money matters, but it is not the only measure of whether something is working.

Sometimes the issue is financial. You gave it a fair chance, put in real effort, and the results simply were not there. Maybe there was not enough demand in your area. Maybe the platform was too competitive. Maybe the timing was wrong. Maybe the pay was too low for the hours required.

Other times, the issue is personal. The money may be there, but the work may not fit your life. If an income source is harming your health, relationships, schedule, safety, or peace of mind, it is worth taking that seriously.

That does not mean you should quit the first time something feels inconvenient. Almost every option in this book will involve some discomfort at the beginning. The first shift, first listing, first client, first interview, or first application may feel awkward. That is normal.

The key is giving something a fair trial before deciding it is a no. One slow afternoon does not tell you much. One item that did not sell, one quiet delivery shift, or one unanswered application is not enough to draw a conclusion. Learn the basics. Put in honest effort. Give it enough time to see whether the problem is the method itself or simply the normal learning curve.

If you have done that and it still is not working, quitting is not failure. It is using the information you have gathered.

Remember what we talked about in Chapter 8. The goal is not to force your life to fit a particular income opportunity. The goal is to find an opportunity that fits your life. If this one does not, take what you learned and move on to something else.

If a friend told you they had honestly tried something for a few weeks and decided it was not a good fit, you probably would not call them a failure. You would probably think they learned something useful and made a reasonable decision.

Offer yourself that same perspective.

Every attempt teaches you something. Sometimes what you learn is, "This works for me." Sometimes what you learn is, "This is not how I want to earn my money." Both are useful. Both move you closer to finding the income source that actually belongs in your life.

9.4 WHEN IT'S ALMOST RIGHT: DECIDING TO PIVOT

The middle case is often the easiest one to misread. Sometimes something is not clearly working, but it is not clearly wrong either. It is close.

That is when a pivot may make sense.

A pivot means the basic idea still seems reasonable, but one part of the execution needs to change. Maybe you tried selling an item on one platform and nothing happened, but a different platform might reach the right buyer. Maybe you tried delivery driving during a slow time of day, but a weekend dinner shift would look completely different. Maybe a freelance pitch went nowhere because of how it was written, who it was sent to, or what you offered, not because the skill itself had no value.

The key difference between quitting and pivoting is that quitting means walking away from that category entirely. Pivoting means adjusting one part of the approach before deciding whether to move on.

It also helps to separate pivoting from scaling. Scaling means doing more of something that is already working. Pivoting means changing something about an approach that is not quite working yet. You are not adding more effort blindly. You are making a specific adjustment to see whether the result improves.

The best pivots are simple. Change one thing at a time if you can. Try a different platform. Adjust your price. Rewrite the listing. Change the hours you work. Offer the service to a different kind of customer. Ask for feedback. Improve the photo, headline, description, or message. The point is not to overhaul everything at once. The point is to test whether one clear change makes the method fit better.

To decide whether a pivot is worth trying, ask yourself: *Was the basic idea reasonable? Did one specific piece seem off? Do I have a clear adjustment I can make? Am I willing to try it one more time?*

If the answer is yes, pivot. Give it another attempt with that one piece changed.

If the honest answer is that nothing about it felt right, even with adjustments, then it may be closer to the quitting case from the previous section. There is no shame in either answer. The only mistake is refusing to look clearly at what the attempt is telling you.

Sometimes the right move is to keep going. Sometimes the right move is to stop. And sometimes the right move is to make one thoughtful adjustment and try again.

9.5 THIS IS YOUR DECISION, NOT ANYONE ELSE'S

The most important thing to carry out of this chapter is this: whether you decide to continue, scale, quit, or pivot, the choice belongs to you.

It does not have to match what a friend would do in the same situation. It does not have to sound impressive when you explain it to someone else. It does not have to meet some imaginary standard of what a person is "supposed" to do.

If scaling feels right, scale. If continuing at the same pace feels right, continue. If quitting is the honest answer, quit. If pivoting makes the most sense, pivot without treating every adjustment as proof that you did something wrong.

Your decision is allowed to change, too. What fits your life this week may not fit a month from now or a year from now. That is not failure. It is simply life changing. A source of income you scaled up may stop fitting once your schedule changes. Something you quit may be worth revisiting later under different circumstances. An approach that needed a pivot once may need another adjustment later.

None of these choices have to be permanent, and none of them need anyone else's approval to be valid.

This is important because a lot of advice makes consistency sound like the highest goal. Consistency is valuable when it is helping you. But sticking with something only because you do not want to look inconsistent is its own trap. So is quitting too early because you are frustrated. The real goal is not to prove that you can stick with one thing forever. The goal is to make an honest decision based on what is actually happening in your life.

This book was never about building the biggest side hustle or finding the perfect income stream. It was about proving something to yourself: that when you needed an extra $100, you were capable of finding a way to make it happen. Along the way, you learned something even more valuable. You discovered what fits your schedule, your responsibilities, your personality, your skills, and your financial situation. Whether you decide to continue, scale, pivot, or move on to something else, you are making that decision based on experience instead of guesswork.

So ask yourself what makes sense now. Not what sounded good three weeks ago. Not what worked for someone else. Not what would look best from the outside.

What fits your life right now?

That is the decision worth trusting.

CHAPTER 10
WHAT THIS WEEK TAUGHT YOU

If you have made it this far and actually tried something, not just read about it or watched videos about it, there is a real chance you have already found your $100.

Maybe you sold a few things from around your house. Maybe you picked up a gig shift or two. Maybe you applied for part-time work, reached out to a potential client, or canceled a stack of subscriptions and watched the math finally start to work. Maybe it did not happen that cleanly. Maybe you are still in the middle of it, adjusting your plan, trying again, or figuring out which option fits best.

Wherever you are right now, this chapter is not really about the hundred dollars anymore. It is about what you learned by taking action.

Because once you prove to yourself that you can do something, the money is only part of the result. You also gain information. You learn what fits your schedule, what drains you, what you are willing to do, and what actually helps. You learn that a financial problem does not always need to be met with panic. Sometimes it can be met with a list, a decision, and one real step.

That lesson can stay with you long after this week is over.

10.1 YOU NOW KNOW SOMETHING YOU DIDN'T KNOW BEFORE

Once you take real action, you stop guessing and start learning.

Maybe the option you tried worked well. Maybe it barely worked. Maybe you decided to keep going, stop, adjust, or try something else. The exact outcome is useful, but it is not the whole point. You now have real information from real action, and that is different from guessing.

Back in the introduction, this book made a simple claim: $100 was never really the goal. It was proof.

Proof that you could look at your situation, choose one step, and follow through. Proof that you could do something instead of only thinking about doing something. If you sold one item, made one phone call, sat through one paid study, drove one shift, canceled one expense, or applied for one opportunity, you created that proof.

It exists now. It is not hypothetical anymore.

Most people are not held back only by a lack of ideas. By the time someone picks up a book like this, they usually already know that selling something, picking up work, or cutting expenses might help. What they do not always know is whether they are the kind of person who will actually act on one of those ideas when money is tight.

Now you know more than you did before.

You know what felt easier than expected. You know what felt harder. You know what fit your schedule and what did not. You know whether a certain kind of work drained you, interested you, paid better than expected, or simply was not worth repeating. Even if the result was messy, you learned something concrete about yourself and your options.

It is worth pausing with that before rushing straight into the next question. It is easy to move immediately into evaluation mode: *Did I make enough? Should I keep going? Was this the right option? Could I have done better?*

Those are fair questions. But underneath them is something steadier: you took action.

That fact does not shrink just because the result was imperfect. A smaller dollar amount does not erase the proof. A messy attempt does not count less than a smooth one. Three adjustments and a near-quit do not make the result less meaningful than something that worked on the first try.

In some ways, a messy result may teach you more. It shows that you can adjust, keep going, and make another decision when the first one does not work exactly as planned. That kind of proof is strong because it is not based on everything going perfectly. It is based on you continuing to act even when the process was imperfect.

10.2 THE STORY FROM CHAPTER 1 DOESN'T HOLD UP ANYMORE

Go back, for a moment, to the specific excuses named early in this book. I don't have time. I don't have any skills anyone would pay for. I don't want to sell my stuff to strangers. I tried something before and it didn't work. I'm too old, or too inexperienced, for this. It's worth checking each of those against what actually happened this week, one at a time, honestly.

If your excuse was time, ask yourself plainly whether you found any, even a little. Most people who actually try something in this book discover that the time existed all along, in the same places it always does: an evening here, a lunch break there, the fifteen minutes that used to disappear into scrolling social media. If you found even a small window and used it, that excuse has already been quietly disproven, whether or not you fully believe it yet.

If your excuse was skills, look honestly at what the method you tried actually required. Did it really demand some specialized training you were missing, or did it mostly ask for a phone, a little time, and a willingness to do something slightly unfamiliar? For almost everyone who tries something in this book, the second description turns out to be closer to true, and the first one turns out to have been the story talking, not the facts.

If your excuse was selling to strangers, and you tried something that didn't actually require that, notice what just happened. You assumed a constraint that was never actually placed on you, and once you looked past it, an entire category of options opened up that had nothing to do with the thing you were avoiding in the first place. And if you did sell something to a stranger and it turned out to be fine, that is worth noticing too, since the discomfort beforehand was almost certainly louder than anything that actually happened during the exchange itself.

If your excuse was a past attempt that didn't pan out, ask what was different this time. Maybe nothing dramatic changed about the method itself. What changed is that you treated this attempt as one data point rather than a verdict, a distinction that matters because it keeps one disappointing try from becoming proof that nothing will ever work.

And if your excuse was age, in either direction, too old or too inexperienced, ask yourself honestly whether anyone you dealt with this week actually cared. For most of the methods in this book, the honest answer is no. Nobody buying a used coffee maker checked your birth year. Nobody ordering food cared how old you were or how many years of experience you had. Most people simply wanted the result they were paying for. The story said your age or experience would matter. The actual week, in most cases, quietly proved otherwise.

None of this means every excuse fully disappears after one attempt. Some genuinely do not, and that is fine. What once looked like an excuse may turn out, after real experience, to be a legitimate preference or boundary. But it is still worth checking honestly, because most people are surprised by how many old stories do not survive contact with one real week of evidence.

10.3 WHAT YOU LEARNED ABOUT TAKING ACTION

Beyond disproving old stories, this week may have taught you something more useful: how you take action when life is already full.

Most people reading this book probably already work hard. You may have a job, a family, school, caregiving responsibilities, bills, errands, and all the ordinary pressure of daily life. The question was never whether you knew how to work. The question was whether you could find one small opening, choose one practical step, and follow through when money was tight.

That is a different kind of skill.

Maybe you learned that you do better with a clear deadline. Maybe you learned that you need to make a decision quickly before you talk yourself out of it. Maybe you discovered that small actions are easier to start than big plans. Maybe you found out that you can use short pockets of time better than you thought. Or maybe you realized that you do not actually want to work more hours at all. Maybe what you really needed was to spend less, not earn more.

That is valuable to know too. There is no rule that says the solution always has to be another job or another side hustle. Sometimes the better answer is making the income you already have go further.

You may also have learned something about what slows you down. Maybe too many options make you freeze. Maybe you spend too much time researching before acting. Maybe you underestimate how much can be done in thirty minutes. Maybe you wait for a perfect plan when a good-enough first step would serve you better.

That information is valuable because it applies beyond this week. The next time money feels tight, you do not have to start from panic. You can remember what helped you move this time. Did listing one item get you started? Did writing down your first three steps help? Did texting one person, filling out one application, or canceling one expense create momentum?

It can help to write a few of these observations down while they are still fresh. Not a long reflection. Just a short note to yourself: what you tried, what helped you start, what slowed you down, what you would repeat, and what you would do differently next time.

Because the real lesson is not only that you found or saved money. It is that you practiced taking action before everything felt perfect. That is something you can use again.

10.4 YOU HAVE MORE OPTIONS THAN YOU THOUGHT

One of the easiest things to believe when money is tight is that you have run out of options.

When an unexpected bill shows up or your bank account is lower than you hoped, it is natural to feel trapped. Your mind focuses on the problem, and before long it can start to feel like there is nothing you can do except hope things somehow get better.

This week challenged that way of thinking.

Instead of asking, "Why is this happening to me?" or "How am I ever going to pay for this?" you started asking a different question: "What can I do today?"

That question changes everything.

It shifts your attention away from the problem and toward possible solutions. Instead of assuming there is nothing you can do, you begin looking for opportunities. You start noticing things you could sell, skills you could use, expenses you could reduce, people you could reach out to, or a few extra hours you could put to good use. You stop waiting for the situation to change and start asking how you can change it.

That does not mean every financial problem will have an easy answer. Sometimes the solution will take time. Sometimes it will require difficult decisions. And sometimes there may not be a perfect answer at all.

But there is a big difference between having no options and not looking for them.

By working through this book, you practiced looking for solutions instead of assuming they did not exist. That habit can help you long after this week's $100 is gone.

The next time life throws you an unexpected expense, your first thought does not have to be, "I'm stuck."

Instead, it can be, "What are my options?"

That simple question is often the first step toward changing your situation.

10.5 THIS DOESN'T END HERE

One of the most valuable things you gained from this week is something you cannot spend.

You proved to yourself that if life throws you an unexpected expense, you know how to respond.

That does not mean every future financial problem will be easy. It does not mean you will never feel stressed about money again. But it does mean you are no longer starting from zero.

The next time your car needs a repair, a medical bill shows up, or your budget feels tighter than expected, you will not be relying only on hope. You already know that you can look for solutions, make a plan, and take action. You have done it before.

That confidence does not disappear just because you are not actively using it.

Think about any other skill you have learned. Riding a bike. Swimming. Driving a car. Even if years pass between using those skills, they come back much faster than they did the first time because you already know you can do them. The same is true here. If you ever need to earn or save extra money again, you will not be learning from scratch. You will be building on experience you already have.

That experience also gives you a choice.

Maybe you decide to keep doing what worked because you enjoy it or because the extra income helps you reach other financial goals. Maybe you continue just enough to build an emergency fund or pay off debt. Maybe you decide to grow it into something much bigger over time.

Or maybe you decide you do not need it anymore.

That is a perfectly good outcome too.

The goal of this book was never to convince you that everyone needs a side hustle forever. It was to help you solve a problem and prove to yourself that you could.

Whatever you choose next is entirely up to you.

The methods may change. Your schedule may change. Your financial situation will almost certainly change. But the experience you gained this week stays with you.

If there is one idea worth carrying forward, let it be this:

When you needed an extra $100, you did not wait for someone else to solve the problem. You made a decision. You looked for solutions. You took action.

That may not seem like a big deal today.

But the next time life surprises you, you will remember that you have already done something difficult once before.

And that may be the most valuable thing you take away from this entire book.

CONCLUSION

Back at the start of this book, I asked you a simple question: If you could put an extra $100 in your pocket this week without starting a business, learning a brand-new skill, or completely changing your schedule, would you do it?

You probably answered yes without much hesitation. Most people do.

The harder question was always the one underneath it. Not whether you wanted an extra $100, but whether you were willing to do something to get it.

That decision, more than any specific method, was the real subject of this book from the very first page.

Everything you've read in these pages comes from real experience, not just something I Googled or pieced together from watching YouTube videos. I've been in situations where I needed extra money, had to get creative, and learned firsthand what actually works and what doesn't. That's why I wanted this book to be practical instead of theoretical. My hope is that something in these pages gives you an idea, a little confidence, or simply reminds you that you have more options than you may think.

If you've made it this far and actually tried something, you already know how the story ends. Maybe you earned the full $100. Maybe you're almost there. Maybe it came together differently than you expected, with a few adjustments along the way.

However it happened, you proved something to yourself that no amount of reading ever could.

You can decide that staying where you are is no longer your only option, and then do something about it.

That is easy to overlook because it is tempting to focus only on the money. Did I make enough? Did I choose the best option? Could I have done it faster?

Those are fair questions.

But a small goal that is actually accomplished is far more valuable than a big goal that never leaves the planning stage. You picked a goal, took action, and moved closer to it. That is something many people never do.

If you have not tried anything yet, and you somehow found yourself reading the conclusion first, go back. Find the chapter that feels most relevant to your situation and take one small step today. No book can do that part for you, but everything you need to get started is already here.

The specific way you earned or saved your $100 was never the point. It was simply the vehicle that helped you prove something much bigger: that when you decide to act, you are capable of following through.

You do not have to turn this into a business. You do not have to chase financial freedom, build an empire, or quit your job. You simply needed an extra $100 and the confidence that comes from knowing you could find a way to get it.

The next time life throws an unexpected expense your way, you will approach it differently. Not because you memorized every idea in this book, but because you know something you did not know before.

You know that when money gets tight, you can stop looking only at the problem and start looking for solutions.

That knowledge stays with you.

So whatever comes next, remember what this week taught you.

You can decide.

You can take action.

And you are capable of finding a way forward.

Go decide.

The rest, you already know how to figure out.

BONUS

300 LEGITIMATE WAYS TO MAKE EXTRA MONEY

I have one final bonus for you.

The following list includes 300 legitimate ways to make extra money. Think of these as ideas to spark your thinking whenever you feel stuck. You won't need all of them. Sometimes all it takes is one idea at the right time.

Sell Things

1. Clothing (Poshmark, Mercari, Depop, ThredUp, Vinted)

2. Shoes (GOAT, StockX, eBay)

3. Designer Handbags (Fashionphile, The RealReal, Rebag)

4. Jewelry (Worthy, eBay)

5. Gold & Silver

6. Watches (Chrono24)

7. Books (BookScouter)

8. Textbooks (BookScouter, Chegg)

9. Phones (Gazelle, Swappa, Decluttr)
10. Laptops (Swappa, eBay)
11. Tablets (Swappa, Gazelle)
12. Cameras & Lenses (MPB, KEH)
13. Video Games (Decluttr, eBay)
14. Game Consoles (Swappa)
15. Furniture (Kaiyo)
16. Appliances
17. Baby Gear (GoodBuy Gear)
18. Sporting Goods (Play It Again Sports, SidelineSwap)
19. Musical Instruments (Reverb)
20. Vinyl Records (Discogs)
21. DVDs / CDs (Decluttr)
22. Collectibles & Toys (eBay, Mercari)
23. Trading Cards (TCGplayer, eBay)
24. Tools & Hardware
25. Craft Supplies (Etsy)
26. Office Equipment
27. Unused Gift Cards (CardCash, Raise)
28. Scrap Metal
29. Wooden Pallets
30. Houseplants & Propagations (Etsy)
31. Baked Goods

32. Homemade Jams & Preserves
33. Firewood
34. Unused Building Materials
35. Comic Books (MyComicShop)
36. Rare Coins (Heritage Auctions)
37. Antiques (Etsy)
38. Facebook Marketplace Flipping
39. Garage / Yard Sale
40. Estate Sale Management

Rent What You Own

41. Spare Room (Airbnb)
42. Entire Home (Airbnb, Vrbo)
43. Car (Turo, Getaround)
44. Driveway / Parking Space (JustPark, SpotHero)
45. Storage Space / Garage (Neighbor)
46. Power Tools & Lawn Equipment (Sparetoolz)
47. Camera Gear (ShareGrid)
48. Electronics & Drones (Fat Llama)
49. Camping & Outdoor Gear (GeerGarage)
50. Baby Equipment (BabyQuip)
51. Party Supplies & Tents
52. Utility / Cargo Trailer
53. Pickup Truck (Fetch Truck, Fluid Truck)

54. RV / Camper (Outdoorsy, RVshare)
55. Boat / Jet Ski (Boatsetter, GetMyBoat)
56. Storage Shed (Neighbor)
57. Office Space / Desks (LiquidSpace, Peerspace)
58. Photography Studio or Event Venue (Peerspace)
59. Backyard for Dogs (Sniffspot)
60. Swimming Pool (Swimply)

Driving & Delivery

61. Rideshare Driving (Uber, Lyft)
62. Food Delivery (DoorDash, Uber Eats, Grubhub)
63. Grocery Shopping & Delivery (Instacart, Shipt)
64. Package Delivery Route (Amazon Flex)
65. Same-Day Local Logistics (Roadie)
66. Convenience Store Delivery (Gopuff)
67. Walmart Grocery Delivery (Spark Driver)
68. Independent Restaurant Delivery
69. Medical Courier (Dropoff)
70. Legal Courier / Document Runner
71. Pharmacy & Prescription Delivery (Medzoomer)
72. Large Item & Furniture Delivery (Lugg, Dolly)
73. Moving Helper (Dolly, TaskRabbit)
74. Airport Shuttle Service
75. Student / Kid Transportation (HopSkipDrive)

76. Peer-to-Peer Laundry Service (Poplin)
77. Corporate Errand Running (TaskRabbit)
78. Senior Transportation Companion (Papa)
79. Advertising On Your Car (Wrapify, Carvertise)
80. Vehicle Relocation Services (Auto Driveaway)

Caregiving & Pet Care

81. Babysitting (Care.com, Sittercity)
82. Nannying (Care.com)
83. After-School Care
84. Mother's Helper
85. Overnight Childcare (Care.com)
86. Senior Companion Care (Papa)
87. Adult Respite Care
88. Pet Sitting & Boarding (Rover)
89. Dog Walking (Rover, Wag!)
90. Cat Sitting / Drop-In Visits (Rover, Meowtel)
91. House Sitting (HouseSitter.com)
92. Plant Watering & House Check-Ins
93. Dog Training
94. Pet Transportation / Taxi (PetBacker)
95. Pet Medication Administration (Rover)
96. Puppy Daycare (Rover)
97. Yard Waste Pickup / Pooper Scooper (DoodyCalls)

98. Litter Box Cleaning Service

99. Pet Grooming / Mobile Bathing

100. Livestock / Farm Sitting

Home & Property Services

101. Standard House Cleaning (TaskRabbit, Handy)

102. Deep Cleaning (Handy)

103. Move-Out / Move-In Cleaning

104. Short-Term Rental / Airbnb Turnover (Turno)

105. Garage Organization

106. Closet & Home Organization (TaskRabbit)

107. Lawn Mowing & Edging (GreenPal)

108. Garden Weeding & Maintenance (TaskRabbit)

109. Leaf Raking & Removal (LawnStarter)

110. Snow Shoveling & Snowblowing (Plowz & Mowz)

111. Pressure Washing (TaskRabbit)

112. Window Washing

113. Gutter Cleaning (LawnStarter)

114. Pool Maintenance & Cleaning

115. Flat-Pack Furniture Assembly (TaskRabbit)

116. TV Mounting & Smart Home Install (TaskRabbit, HelloTech)

117. Handyman Work (Thumbtack)

118. Interior Painting & Accent Walls (TaskRabbit)

119. Exterior Fence / Deck Staining (Thumbtack)

120. Packing & Boxing for Moves (TaskRabbit)
121. Unpacking & House Setup
122. Junk Removal & Hauling
123. Holiday Decorating
124. Christmas Light Installation
125. Air Filter & Smoke Detector Battery Replacement Service

Teaching, Tutoring & Coaching

126. K-12 Subject Tutoring (Wyzant)
127. Reading & Literacy Tutoring (Wyzant)
128. SAT / ACT Test Prep (Wyzant)
129. Online Conversational English Teaching (Cambly, VIPKid)
130. Foreign Language Tutoring (Preply, italki)
131. Music Lessons (TakeLessons)
132. Art & Drawing Lessons (Outschool)
133. In-Home Cooking Lessons
134. Photography Techniques & Editing Lessons
135. Personal Fitness Training (FindYourTrainer)
136. Yoga / Pilates Instruction
137. Youth Swim Lessons
138. Private Sports Coaching (CoachUp)
139. Driving School Instructor
140. Resume & LinkedIn Profile Writing (Fiverr, Upwork)
141. Interview Prep & Mock Interviews

142. Career Coaching (BetterUp)
143. College Admissions Essay Coaching
144. Public Speaking Coaching (Upwork)
145. Computer Literacy for Seniors
146. Basic Financial Literacy Coaching
147. Chess Instruction (Outschool)
148. Sewing, Knitting, or Crafting Lessons
149. Kids' Coding / STEM Tutoring (Outschool)
150. Specialized Corporate Software Training (Upwork)

Freelancing & Creative Services

151. Freelance Article & Blog Writing (Upwork, Fiverr, ProBlogger)
152. Copywriting (Upwork)
153. Content Editing (Upwork, Reedsy)
154. Proofreading (ProofreadingPal)
155. Graphic Design (99designs, Fiverr)
156. Logo & Brand Identity Design (Fiverr)
157. UI / UX Web Design (Upwork)
158. Front-End Web Development (Upwork, Toptal)
159. Virtual Assistant Services (Belay)
160. Bookkeeping (QuickBooks ProAdvisor)
161. Data Entry (Clickworker)
162. Audio Transcription (Rev, TranscribeMe)
163. Document Translation (Gengo)

164. Voice-Over Work (Voices.com, Voice123)
165. Podcast Audio Editing (Fiverr)
166. Video Editing (Upwork, Fiverr)
167. Event & Portrait Photography
168. Real Estate Photography & Virtual Tours
169. Commercial Product Photography (Fiverr)
170. Social Media Management (Upwork)
171. Short-Form Video Content Creation (Billo)
172. Search Engine Optimization Consulting (Upwork)
173. Email Marketing Campaign Management (Upwork)
174. Online Course Structure Creation
175. Pitch Deck & Presentation Design (Upwork)

Traditional Part-Time Jobs

176. Retail Sales Associate
177. Cashier
178. Restaurant Server
179. Bartender
180. Barista
181. Line Cook / Prep Cook
182. Warehouse Associate
183. Stocking Associate
184. Hotel Housekeeping
185. Hotel Night Auditor / Front Desk

186. Movie Theater Crew
187. Grocery Clerk
188. General Administrative Temp (Robert Half)
189. Virtual Customer Service Agent (Liveops, Arise)
190. Inbound Call Center Representative
191. Office Receptionist
192. Substitute Teacher (Swing Education)
193. Bank Teller
194. Unarmed Security Guard (Securitas)
195. School Crossing Guard
196. Package Handler
197. Retail Inventory Counter (RGIS)
198. Stadium Concessions Worker
199. Lifeguard
200. Parking Lot Attendant

Event & Entertainment Work

201. Day-Of Wedding Assistant
202. Event Setup Crew
203. Event Teardown & Clean Crew
204. Photo Booth Attendant
205. Party Face Painter
206. Balloon Artist / Decorator
207. DJ Assistant / Audio Tech Runner

208. Concert / Theatre Usher
209. Ticket Scanner / Gate Staff
210. Event Parking Valet
211. Music / Arts Festival Staff
212. Trade Show / Convention Worker
213. County Fair / Carnival Worker
214. Sporting Event Guest Services
215. Casino Party Dealer
216. Trivia / Bingo Night Host (Geeks Who Drink)
217. Holiday Performer
218. Easter Bunny Performer
219. Mascot Performer
220. Catering Server / Banquet Staff
221. Brand Ambassador
222. Escape Room Game Master
223. Art and Sip Party Instructor
224. Tour Guide
225. Event Coat Check Attendant

Handmade, Food & Creative Products

226. Handmade Jewelry (Etsy)
227. Crocheted Plushies & Wearables (Etsy)
228. Knitted Accessories (Ravelry, Etsy)
229. Woodworked Crafts & Small Furniture (Etsy)

230. Custom Laser Engraved Gifts (Etsy)
231. 3D Printed Objects / Models (Etsy, eBay)
232. Hand-Poured Soy Candles (Etsy)
233. Artisan Soap & Bath Bombs (Etsy)
234. Custom Sublimation Tumblers & Mugs (Etsy)
235. Handmade Greeting Cards (Etsy)
236. Curated Home Decor (Etsy)
237. Custom Embroidery & Monogramming (Etsy)
238. Clothing & Sewing Alterations
239. Custom Celebration Cakes
240. Custom Decorated Sugar Cookies
241. Private Meal Prep Chef
242. Fine Dining Private Dinner Chef (Cozymeal)
243. Farmers Market Farm Produce Vendor
244. Seasonal Holiday Treat Boxes
245. Printable Downloads / Trackers (Etsy)
246. Printable / Digital Coloring Pages (Etsy)
247. Digital Planners (Etsy)
248. Digital Wall Art Prints (Etsy)
249. Bespoke Wedding Invitations & Stationery (Etsy, Minted)
250. Custom Vinyl Decals & Stickers (Etsy)

Automotive Services

251. Mobile Exterior Detailing

252. Interior Deep Clean Detailing
253. Headlight Restoration (Thumbtack)
254. Boat Marine Cleaning & Waxing
255. RV Exterior Washing & Detailing
256. Commercial Fleet Washing
257. Classic / Luxury Vehicle Photography
258. Local Car Transport / Dealership Shuttling
259. Mobile Oil Change Service
260. Mobile Brake Pad Replacement
261. Car Battery Delivery & Installation
262. Windshield Chip Repair
263. Home Tire Rotation & Pressure Checks
264. Residential Driveway Trash Can Washing
265. Motorcycle Detailing

Research, Testing & Bureaucratic Services

266. Plasma Donation (BioLife, CSL Plasma)
267. Paid Clinical Trials (ClinicalTrials.gov)
268. University Paid Research Studies
269. Paid In-Person Focus Groups (FocusGroup.com)
270. Mystery Shopping (BestMark)
271. In-Home Product Testing (UserTesting)
272. Website User Experience Testing (UserTesting)
273. Mobile App Beta Testing (UserTesting)

274. Online Consumer Surveys (Prolific, Survey Junkie, Swagbucks)

275. Remote Search Quality Evaluator (Telus International, Appen)

276. Mobile Notary Public & Loan Signing Agent

277. Custom Travel Itinerary Planning (Thumbtack, Fiverr)

278. Professional Line Standing (TaskRabbit)

279. Personal Lifestyle Concierge (TaskRabbit)

280. Smart TV & Home Theater Tech Setup (HelloTech)

281. Home Printer & Networking Troubleshooting (HelloTech)

282. Whole-Home Wi-Fi Mesh Network Setup (HelloTech)

283. Vintage Photo & Slide Digitizing

284. Physical Document Filing & Organization (TaskRabbit)

285. Genealogy & Family Tree Research (Fiverr)

Digital & Remote Micro-Tasks

286. AI Large Language Model Training & Evaluation (DataAnnotation.tech, Outlier.ai)

287. Audio / Voice Data Collection for AI (Appen)

288. Image & Video Data Labeling (Scale AI)

289. Content Moderation for Forums & Social Spaces (ModSquad)

290. Captions & Subtitle Creation (Rev)

291. Digital Coupon / Cashback Optimization (Ibotta)

292. Website Domain Flipping (GoDaddy Auctions)

293. Stock Video / B-Roll Footage Submissions (Shutterstock, Pond5)

Specialized Niche Consulting

294. Google Business Profile Optimization for Small Businesses

295. Pinterest Account Management for Bloggers (Upwork)

296. Notion Workspace Setup & Template Building (Gumroad)

297. Facebook / Meta Ads Management for Local Businesses (Upwork)

298. Airbnb Listing Optimization & Description Copywriting (Fiverr)

299. Podcast Launch Consulting & Distribution Setup (Upwork)

300. Remote Tech Support for Small Non-Profits

www.ingramcontent.com/pod-product-compliance
Lightning Source LLC
LaVergne TN
LVHW022056200926
848481LV00003B/946
* 9 7 9 8 9 9 3 3 2 9 2 6 0 *